CASE STUDIES IN

CULTURAL ANTHROPOLOGY

GENERAL EDITORS
George and Louise Spindler
STANFORD UNIVERSITY

THE KAPAUKU
PAPUANS
OF WEST NEW GUINEA

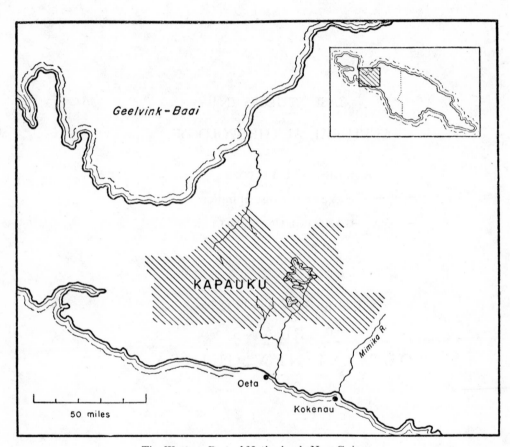

The Western Part of Netherlands New Guinea.

THE KAPAUKU
PAPUANS
OF WEST
NEW GUINEA

Second Edition

BY

LEOPOLD POSPISIL

Yale University

HOLT, RINEHART AND WINSTON

NEW YORK   CHICAGO   SAN FRANCISCO   DALLAS

MONTREAL   TORONTO   LONDON   SYDNEY

Library of Congress Cataloging in Publication Data

Pospisil, Leopold J.
   The Kapauku Papuans of West New Guinea.

   Bibliography: p. 127
   1. Kapauku (Papuan people)   I. Title.
DU744.35.K34P67   1978   301.29'95'1   77-25981
ISBN 0-03-041621-3

Foreword

About the Series

These case studies in cultural anthropology are designed to bring to students in the social sciences insights into the richness and complexity of human life as it is lived in different ways and in different places. They are written by men and women who have lived in the societies they write about, and who are professionally trained as observers and interpreters of human behavior. The authors are also teachers, and in writing their books they have kept the students who will read them foremost in their minds. It is our belief that when an understanding of ways of life very different from one's own is gained, abstractions and generalizations about social structure, cultural values, subsistence techniques, and the other universal categories of human social behavior become meaningful.

About the Author

Leopold J. Pospisil is professor of anthropology at Yale University and also associate curator at the Peabody Museum. He holds a Ph.D. in anthropology from Yale, and an M.A. from the University of Oregon. He also has a law degree from the Charles University of Prague, and studied philosophy at Masaryk's University in Ludwigsburg. He was a lawyer in Czechoslovakia for a brief time (1947–1948), but had to escape from his country after the communist *coup d'état*. He has done field work with the Kapauku, the Nunamiut Eskimo, the Hopi Indians, and in a Tirolean village. He has written four books, *Kapauku Papuans and Their Law*, *Kapauku Papuan Economy*, *Anthropology of Law*, and *Ethnology of Law* and has published widely in professional journals. He is a Fellow in the American Anthropological Association, and a member of Sigma Xi, and the Czechoslovak Society of Arts and Sciences in America, and the Connecticut Archeological Society.

About the Book

As Dr. Pospisil points out in his introductory chapter, the Kapauku, a Papuan society in its pristine aboriginal state when studied first by him in 1954–1955, dramatically contradicts the preconceived ideas and clichés "addressed by the West to primitive peoples in general." This society, characterized by a form of "primitive capitalism," has well-developed trade, money, and legal systems. It provides even greater vertical mobility in its socioeconomic structure than does ours. Its legal system operates with at least 121 abstract prohibitions and a body of knowledge about previous disputes and settlements that provides guidance for deviations from the rules. And the Kapauku are preoccupied with quantification and have a highly developed numerical system.

Not only in these respects is the picture of the Kapauku drawn by Dr. Pospisil compelling and fascinating. Where else would one find a society where an eleven-year-old son can beat his own father for refusal to pay back a debt, leaving the father happy because he knows from this that his son will be a great businessman? Or a society where pig feasts and *ugaa* songs combine to provide an event that is like "going to a dance, singing, listening to new poetry, witnessing disputes and matchmaking, reading the newspaper, and participating in a cocktail party—all at the same time"? Or where the creator is viewed as omnipotent, omniscient, omnipresent, and nonexistent?

There are many surprises in this case study. The author gives the reader the details that are necessary to a full understanding of the complex Kapauku society but also succeeds in enlivening his picture of it with observations that convey the esoteric, dramatic, but strangely familiar quality of Kapauku behavior. We leave the reader to his own discoveries from this point. He will find the experience captivating and instructive.

About the Second Edition

Though it is regarded as highly desirable by anthropologists to do long-range studies of single societies, such studies are relatively rare. We are fortunate that Leopold Pospisil has returned to study the Kapauku Papuans several times over a twenty-year period. The benefits of such a long-term study are obvious, and are made particularly important because the baseline for change for the Kapauku, and for the anthropologist studying them, was the native culture and social structure literally untouched by the outside world and its civilization.

Professor Pospisil has succeeded in compacting his observations on change for the Kapauku into a manageable chapter. In this relatively brief addition to this case study he discusses changes in socio-political alliances, in the incest taboo, in agricultural patterns, in population, and in the nature of a reactive movement consequent to contact with the outside world.

Though the results of intensive contact with the outside world for the Kapauku are not without some sad features, one must judge these results, in the overall balance, as positive. Perhaps this is so, in part, because the individualistic, profit-oriented Kapauku found Western capitalism congenial and began very quickly and effectively to exploit its possibilities. Professor Pospisil discusses this relationship as well.

GEORGE AND LOUISE SPINDLER
General Editors

Stanford, California
1977

Preface to First Edition

The research among the Kapauku of Western New Guinea that forms the basis for this book was conducted during three separate periods of investigation. The first and longest (September 1954 to November 1955) was generously financed by the Ford Foundation; the two subsequent restudies during the summers of 1959 and 1962 were made possible by grants awarded by the American Philosophical Society and the Social Science Research Council. The three institutions, however, are not to be understood as necessarily approving by virtue of their grants any of the statements made or views expressed in this book.

I wish to convey my gratitude for the assistance in inland transportation, protection, and general support to the administration of Netherlands New Guinea, and in particular to its able officer R. den Haan. For help with learning the Kapauku language I am indebted to Marion Doble. Finally, I wish to thank my colleague Prof. Kwang-Chih Chang for assistance in expediting the manuscript to the editor, and Anne F. Wilde for her editorial services.

LEOPOLD POSPISIL

New Haven, Conn.
1963

Preface to Second Edition

In the career of an anthropologist field work plays such a dominant role that it is often assumed that the people whom an anthropologist studies, or at least the area in which he conducts his research, constitutes the object of his enduring interest—indeed that because of his interest in a specific people or part of the world he became an anthropologist. That might be accurate for some of my colleagues, but it is not true for all. I myself became interested in the problems of social control and law and came into anthropology to study peoples unrelated culturally to the Western tradition in order to arrive at a comparative theory of law. New Guinea and the Kapauku were simply chosen for study because of their isolation. In order to get a dynamic picture of the culture and its law I planned a long-term research, with periodic returns to the Kapauku, for a time span of at least ten years. The first edition (Chapters 1–5) of this book represent a cross-section of the aboriginal Kapauku culture of 1954–1955, uninfluenced by civilization; the added chapter in this volume gives to the study a time depth by discussing the changes that have affected Kapauku society for the last twenty years.

My return to the Kapauku has not only been most rewarding intellectually, in terms of my attempt to better understand social control and law cross-culturally, but it has also been very rewarding personally. My return to the people has reinforced the old bonds of friendship and adoptive relationships, and has moved me, I hope only in my heart, away from objectivity and neutrality.

LEOPOLD POSPISIL

New Haven, Conn.
1977

Contents

A Kapauku headman delivering a political speech.

A woman and adolescent girls.

Above: ema, *the Kapauku dance house.*

Above: a scene from a Kapauku pig feast.

Kapauku sweet potato and sugar cane gardens.

Introduction

THE KAPAUKU PAPUANS are mountain people who belong to one of several tribes whose members inhabit the Central Highlands of Western New Guinea. It is estimated that the number of the Kapauku population approaches 45,000 individuals. They live in a territory situated in the west-central part of the Highlands, located between 135°25′ and 137° east longitude and 3°25′ and 4°10′ south latitude. Their country, most of which lies 1500 meters* above sea level, is composed of rugged mountain chains (some of whose peaks attain an altitude of 4000 meters) and deep valleys. The most spectacular feature of the country's topography are three large lakes called Paniai, Tage, and Tigi. They lie in the northeastern part of the Kapauku country, in a line from north to south. To the Western world this system of the three water reservoirs is known as Wissel Lakes, named after their discoverer who spotted them from his small plane in the year 1936. To the west lies a residuum of a fourth old lake—the flat, swampy Kamu Valley, dotted with small lakes and drained by numerous streams that flow into the main river of the valley, the Edege. Water from all these lakes and streams ultimately flows into the Jawei River, which carries it south into the Indian Ocean. The climate of this region may be described as mild, with little seasonal change. The daily temperatures in the shade reach about 20° C (68° F). The nights are cold and toward morning the mercury may drop to 6° C (41° F), or even lower. Although there are no regular, well-defined rainy seasons, the precipitation is abundant all year around, but especially in the months of June, August, and September (annual rainfall is about 2500 millimeters; 98.5 inches).

Influenced by topography, elevation, and the human agent the flora of this region forms five distinct vegetation zones: tropical rain forest, mountain moss forest, Alpine scrub and grassland, swampy grasslands of the valley floors, and secondary forest. The tropical rain forest covers the mountain slopes to an elevation of 2000 meters. It consists of a great variety of hardwood ever-

---

* The metric system is used throughout this book. 1500 meters is equal to 1640 yards. See the conversion table at the end of the Glossary.

greens, of which the oaks and beeches especially are prominent. The undergrowth is often composed of many varieties of ferns, pandanus palms, shrubs, and vines. Above the 2000-meter level one enters the zone of the moss forest. Here there are fewer trees, and the undergrowth is less thick, showing a great abundance of various types of moss, lichens, and fern. The steep mountain slopes as well as the lofty summits are covered with an Alpine vegetation, composed of stunted shrubs, grasses, and various herbs. The floors of the deep valleys are, as a rule, swampy and covered with grass, fern, and reed growth. The secondary forests, a by-product of the native agricultural practices, are composed of several varieties of fast-growing willowlike trees, and of dense vine and grassy undergrowth.

The native fauna of New Guinea is characterized by an almost complete absence of placental mammals. Except for a few species of rats and bats and a wild pig, the island's animal life consists of several types of marsupials (such as bandicoots, phallangers—opossums and cuscus, wallabies, and tree kangaroos), lizards, amphibians, and a great variety of insects and birds. Of the latter the most prominent are the birds of paradise, parrots, hawks, herons, hornbills, swifts, and the flightless cassowary bird.

The name Kapauku has been given to the people by their southern neighbors who inhabit the southwestern coastal territory, which includes the Mimika, Oeta, and Kokenau regions. While the Moni Papuans who live northeast of the Kapauku call them *Ekari*, the Kapauku refer to themselves as *Me*, which means "the people." Physically they belong to a composite race called Mountain Papuans. Because of their short stature they have been often erroneously classified as Oceanic Negritos. The males of the Kamu Valley average 151.2 centimeters in height, while the average female is only 142.1 centimeters tall. Their heads are brachycephalic (male index, 80; female index, 81) and their faces are broad (male index, 78; female index, 76). Their skin color varies from deep, dark brown to light bronze. The light skin color of some small babies approaches the pigmentation of the Caucasians. Their hair, whose form may be kinky, curly, or wavy, is dark brown. About 35 percent of the children are red-blond, but this color has darkened by about the age of fifteen years, although some individuals retain the reddish hair color until their early thirties. The facial aspect of this people is fierce and strongly reminds one of the Australian Aborigine. Heavy brow-ridges overhang broad noses that have straight bridges and deeply depressed roots and fleshy tips. The septum invariably protrudes downward, thus enabling the native to perforate and adorn it with huge boar tusk nose plugs. The wild look of the Kapauku male is further accentuated by a wreath of black beard left growing on each side of his massive jaw. His thick, but not everted lips are often spread in a broad grin, thus dispelling the impression of ferocity and revealing two rows of healthy, large, white teeth. The older Kapauku males show a pronounced frontal baldness as well as a heavy growth of body hair. Generally speaking, their bodies are muscular and well proportioned.

Isolated from the outside world by high mountain ranges and extensive lowland tropical rain forests and swamps, the Kapauku led their aboriginal lives undisturbed by the spreading Western civilization until 1938. At that time a Dutch government outpost was created at Paniai Lake and a white administration officer stationed there. However, this contact was short lived because of the Japanese assault against the islands of the southwestern Pacific. After hiding for some time the administration officer departed from New Guinea thus leaving the natives again without a connection with the white man until 1946. At that time a new government outpost was established at Paniai Lake, and a few Catholic and Protestant missionaries arrived to see to the spiritual welfare of the people. All the personnel and supplies have to be flown into the Kapauku country by planes that, until recently, had to land on Paniai Lake.

The three separate field periods, on which this book is based, together total approximately twenty-two months of research time. I spent fourteen months among the Kapauku in 1954 and 1955, when I studied the native language and culture and analyzed the people's primitive law. During this first field period I was fortunate enough to study the Kapauku society of the Kamu Valley at a time when it had not yet met Western civilization or been brought under its legal control. Thus I had a unique opportunity to be exposed to an untouched Stone-Age Papuan society and to study its primitive political institutions in action. During this first stay in New Guinea I even witnessed two native wars, fought with bows and arrows.

This book presents basically the aboriginal conditions as they existed during my first field session. Consequently, it is written in the "historical present," which means that the reader is confronted with the Kapauku society in the present tense, as though the people's mode of life had not changed since 1955. The subsequent two research periods during the two summers of 1959 and 1962 furnish this book with only subsidiary data. The main purpose of the two restudies of the Kapauku society was to analyze acculturation and culture change resulting from changes in native legal systems as well as from the imposition of European legal codes.

The following account of the Kapauku culture will present the reader with concise statements on the native economy and technology, social organization, political and legal structure, and religious and ceremonial life. The final chapter summarizes the main characteristics of the people's attitudes, philosophical outlook, and way of life. The book is intended to convey a comprehensive picture of a Papuan society that, in several respects, contradicts the dogmatic statements, preconceived ideas, and clichés addressed by the West to primitive peoples in general. For example, instead of a "primitive communism," the Kapauku economy resembles something that may be better labeled as "primitive capitalism." Instead of collectivism we find here an extreme type of individualism, and instead of a qualitative orientation—an obsession with quantification manifest in an emphasis on counting and in a highly developed numerical system. One of the most primitive technologies on earth is combined here with a complex and rather sophisticated type of true money economy. A "typical" preoccupation with the supernatural and ritual is replaced among these "primitives" by a secular and profit-motivated outlook on life. The Kapauku certainly do not conform to the popular Western belief in the "prelogical mentality" of the primitives. Thus the present book may assist in tearing down hypothetical barrier of qualitative differences which has been erected by some Western writers between the so-called "primitive" and the "advanced" or "civilized" societies.

1

Economy

Food Production

I N THEIR ENVIRONMENT of high mountains, deep valleys, virgin rain forests, swampy grassland areas, and mild climate the Kapauku Papuans of
the Kamu Valley make their living by cultivating several plants and by
pig breeding. Because of the scarcity of large game, hunting and trapping are
relatively unimportant and are practiced more as forms of sport and enjoyment
than as serious economic endeavor. In the Kamu Valley, which has been
stripped of its low-altitude forests, the larger animals of the region such as
cassowary birds, wild boars, and large marsupials have retreated to the dense
jungle on the more remote mountain slopes. As a result, hunting and trapping
of any economic consequence are limited to small birds, bats, and rats. Fishing
and gathering provide the Papuans with additional proteins and vegetable material. In their fishless rivers and lakes the native women net crayfish, dragonfly
larvae, tadpoles, and water bugs. In addition they collect many species of insects, several types of frogs, a large lizard, bird eggs, and a large variety of
greens and fruits.

Since breeding and fattening pigs depend on the harvest of sweet potatoes (the staple of the native diet), agriculture assumes an undisputed key
role in the native food production. However, its significance transcends the
area of nutrition, and even the field of the native economy. The culture of the
Kapauku is wealth oriented. This means that the highest prestige in this society and the highest status of political and legal leadership are achieved not
through heritage, bravery in warfare, or knowledge and achievements in religious ceremonialism, but through accumulation and redistribution of capital.
The major and often the only source of capital, generally in the form of shell
money, is successful pig breeding. Thus indirectly, agriculture, by providing
food for the pigs, not only creates wealth but also provides a basis for acquiring
political and legal powers.

AGRICULTURE   The Kamu Valley has two different types of terrain. First there are the steep slopes of the mountains that surround the valley, characterized by numerous limestone walls and cliffs and a relatively thin layer of alkaline, coarse, yellowish soil that is rich in minerals and organic material. This sloping and well-drained area is covered with secondary forests and dense ground vegetation. The floor of the valley, in contrast, is flat, devoid of rocks, and has a deep layer of sedimentary, acid, heavy, black soil that can be classified as silt loam and clay loam. This valley soil is poorly drained and is not so rich in minerals as the mountain slopes. The Kapauku have adjusted their agriculture to these two sets of land conditions by applying two different agricultural methods. On the mountain slopes they use a shifting cultivation technique, which they combine with an emphasis upon extensive rather than intensive production. The man, with the help of his wife, first clears the underbrush from a selected site. Then he cuts down the forest with his stone ax and introduced machete, trims off the branches, and processes the wood so that it can be used to build a fence. When this work is finished, the uprooted underbrush and the branches form a continuous layer of dry debris that covers the garden area. In order to protect the crops from destruction by marauding wild boars and domesticated pigs the Kapauku farmer must build a sturdy fence around his property. The mountain slopes with their numerous boulders, stone terraces, and rocky outcrops require a complex type of fence called *wageedaa:* horizontal poles, tied with rattan or vine to posts standing far apart, bridge the stony patches and form a strong barrier. Building such a structure is an arduous task; one section of this fence, about 4.20 meters long, requires on the average, two hours and forty minutes of hard labor. After this fence is completed and the plot safely enclosed, the native farmer, often aided by his wife, removes the dry debris from the vicinity of the fence and sets the whole garden area on fire by means of a fire saw consisting of a forked wooden stick against which a flexible bamboo section is rubbed. The worker steps on the stick, after he has passed the bamboo section underneath it. He then holds the bamboo by both ends and quickly pulls it back and forth, the friction igniting a tinder of dried banana leaves. The garden is usually set afire at the lower edge so that the whole area is swept by a single, spectacular blaze. Since the surrounding jungle is always damp from the frequent tropical rains, there is no danger that the fire will spread into it. With the firing process the man's work is completed, and the female takes over the care of the newly created garden. On the next day she appears with bundles of shoots of sweet potato vines, which she plants in shallow holes by means of a dibble stick. The abundant moisture and sometimes daily tropical rains cause the shoots to root and grow fast. Unfortunately, the rains also stimulate the growth of weeds. It is the woman's task also to keep the gardens clean and to weed them at least three times during their growing period. Only such care assures an adequate harvest. Most of the harvesting is again accomplished by the woman who digs out the ripe tubers with a short, pointed digging stick. The harvest of sweet potatoes is a protracted affair. A woman harvests daily only as many tubers as she needs for feeding herself, her children, her husband, and her husband's pigs. Consequently, sweet potatoes are dug from the same garden for a prolonged period of time. Usually the whole area is gone over three times before all the tubers are extracted and the plot is abandoned as fallow land to the pigs and the jungle.

The soil of the valley floor requires a different method of tilling. This land is flat, and its cover, being devoid of trees, consists primarily of grass, reeds, and an occasional shrub. In cultivating this land the farmer makes use of two different methods. One, which may be called intensive shifting cultivation, consists of simply clearing the grass from the area by uprooting and burning it, erecting a fence around the plot, and providing the area with a few deep drainage ditches. In a garden plot thus prepared sweet potatoes or a variety of different cultigens such as sugar cane, taro, bananas, several types of greens, cucumbers, gourds, and native beans are planted. Whereas digging the ditches and building the fences are a man's work, weeding is primarily the task of a woman. Both sexes share in clearing the plot, planting, and harvesting the various crops, but certain cultigens are the responsibility of the women, and others are cared for primarily by the men. Although this method—burning off the surface vegetation and a discontinuous cropping that involves fallowing periods that are longer than those of the actual cultivation—resembles the cultivation on the mountain slopes and has to be classified with it as shifting cultivation, it nevertheless shows important differences. Unlike the mountain slopes, the flat land of the valley with its deep soil permits a large variety of domesticated plants in addition to the staple sweet potatoes. Owing to the different vegetative cover and a poor drainage the process of making a garden also shows significant differences from that employed on the sloping terrain. Since there are no trees the natives do not have the difficult task of cutting them down, but this is compensated for by the fact that wood for the necessary fences has to be cut in the distant forests and transported to the valley plot. A simple fence of *weedaa* type is constructed in the valley; poles are driven into the soft ground next to each other and lashed to two horizontal crossbeams. Compared with the complex fence constructed on the mountains, the simple valley type saves the laborer approximately thirty hours of work on a fence 120 meters long. There are several other significant differences between the mountain slopes and the valley shifting cultivation. The farmer must provide his valley plots with adequate drainage; he usually has to dig with a wooden spadelike tool a ditch approximately 75 centimeters deep and 50 centimeters wide around his rectangular plot. A drainage construction 120 meters long requires approximately thirty-one hours of the worker's time. For this additional labor the farmer is rewarded by higher yields and by the fact that through crop rotation he is able to cultivate the same area several times in a sequence before it must revert to fallow land. On the sloping mountainous terrain a single crop of sweet potatoes has to be followed by a fallow period of eight to twelve years.

In addition to the two types of shifting cultivation the Kapauku use in their valley gardens a third agricultural method that differs from these in several important respects. These differences are so basic that the method cannot be called shifting cultivation; this method, which I call "intensive complex cultivation," is characterized by a laborious turning over of the soil with a spadelike tool in such a way that a system of rectangular beds is carefully formed with drainage ditches surrounding each of them. These beds are artificially fertilized with fresh plant material (such as grass, reed, leaves) or with rotted leaves and moss. After every crop a new layer of fertilizer is placed on top of the bed and is covered with washed-down mud from the ditches; cultivation of such a garden plot can therefore continue almost indefinitely. The dibble stick, so typical of the shifting cultivation, is not employed in this method. Also, because the green vegetation is used for fertilizing the area, the ground growth is usually not cleared by fire. In these raised beds the Kapauku grow root crops such as sweet potatoes and the introduced manioc and Irish potatoes, and a type of spinachlike green, *idaja (Amaranthus hybridus)*.

In order to give the reader an idea of the economic effectiveness of the three methods I shall compare the yields from, and the amount of labor expended on, an area of 900 square meters cultivated by each of the methods. Since the sweet potato is the most important staple, and is grown by all three methods, it seems logical to select for the comparison gardens cultivated with this plant. With respect to the amount of labor spent on cultivating an area of 900 square meters the two intensive methods applied to the valley gardens prove to be considerably more onerous than the extensive shifting cultivation of the mountain slopes. The latter requires only about 260 hours of the laborer's time, the intensive shifting cultivation requires about 300 hours, and the intensive complex cultivation requires about 450 hours on areas of the same size. The rewards correspond roughly to the time spent. While a mountain garden of 900 square meters yields approximately 380 kilograms of sweet potatoes, the intensive shifting cultivation of the same area in the valley produces 560 kilograms, and the intensive complex cultivation compensates the cultivator with 640 kilograms of tubers for his hard work.

In their gardens the Kapauku Papuans cultivate a rather surprisingly large variety of plants. By far the most important is the sweet potato, which almost always covers at least 90 percent of the total garden area. Next in importance come sugar cane (about 5 percent of the total area), taro (about 2 percent), *idaja* (about 1.5 percent), edible cane *(Saccharum edule)* (about 1.2 percent), and bananas (about 0.3 percent). In addition to these crops the Kapauku "kitchen gardens," which are usually located near the houses, produce a large variety of vegetables on areas that figure only as a fraction of 1 percent of the total cultivated land. So we find in these gardens a variety of greens, such as *jatu (Setaria palmaefolia), petai* (an introduced variety of lettuce), *kagame (Solanum nigrum), dade (Hibiscus manihot), damuwe (Oenanthe javanica)*, and *digioo (Rungia klosii)*. A few additional root crops such as the introduced manioc, Irish potatoes, and yams augment the inventory of these gardens. In addition to these cultigens the natives also grow native beans, bottle gourds, native squash, ginger, and a few introduced plants such as maize, tomatoes, string beans, onions, and chili peppers.

A cursory glance at the enumeration of the cultivated plants and the areas on which they are grown reveals the overwhelming importance of the main native staple—the sweet potato. About 90 percent of all the garden land of the Kapauku is planted with this crop. All the plots on the mountains slopes, and about 60 percent of the valley gardens are devoted to its cultivation. Translated into the amount of effort spent on cultivating the various types of crops, the sweet potato claims seven eighths of the time spent by the Kapauku on all agricultural labor. In 1955 I calculated the total yields of the gardens of the village of Botukebo. The results showed beyond doubt the great dependence of the native economy on sweet potatoes. In a period of eight months the natives harvested about 138,000 kilograms of these tubers. In contrast to this large harvest taro yielded in kilograms only 2500, manioc about 57, bananas about 70, and the *idaja* green about 500. The role of the sweet potato is not limited to furnishing the natives with their main source of food; because the growing root crops are often sold, and because substantial quantities of the harvested tubers are fed to the pigs, the sweet potato is the only cultivated plant that becomes a source of capital for the native cultivator. Since the sale of pigs and of pork constitute the main income of a native, the sweet potatoes must ultimately be held responsible for the creation of wealth in this Papuan society. As we shall see in the following chapters, Kapauku place a great value upon wealth. Only a rich man becomes a political leader and a judicial authority in his group. Consequently the pig and the sweet potato play a pivotal role in the wealth-oriented Kapauku society.

All the Kapauku agricultural land is owned individually. My investigation of the village of Botukebo revealed a high variation in the size of cultivated areas owned by the individual gardeners. Several hypotheses may be advanced for this variability. One may propose that the amount of land cultivated by a particular gardener reflects the number of his dependents who help to cultivate it and who derive their subsistence from its yields. The amount of cultivated land may also be related to the wealth of its owner, or to the sum of the wealth of all individuals who partake in the tilling of the soil. Also personal attributes of the cultivator may greatly influence the amount of garden land he cultivates. If we make an inquiry into the correlation between the size of the group who depend for their livelihood on the produce of an area, and the size of such an area, a problem presents itself: which of three different groups should be considered? There is the family (nuclear and polygynous) of the landowner, or his "gardening unit" that comprises all the persons (with their dependents) who regularly till the same land, or the whole household, that is a group of people who share a common residence and who plan their consumption in common. In order to decide which of these three different groups is most pertinent to the size of its cultivated area I have correlated the size of individual families, gardening units, and households of the village of Botukebo with the amount of land cultivated by each of these groups. The results showed beyond doubt that it is the Kapauku household whose size, which shows a correlation of 0.56 with its pertinent garden land, influences most profoundly the extent of the cultivated area. In contrast, similar correlations between the sizes of particular families and gardening units, and their cultivated land areas showed lower correlation indices of 0.22 and 0.38 respectively. Since consumption is planned on the household level, and because this planning affects production, it is not surprising that it is the size of the household that shows the most significant correlation with the size of the cultivated area.

It may be further hypothesized that it is not merely the size of a household that influences significantly the amount of the land cultivated by its members but that a specific composition of such a group (in terms of sex, age, and marital status of its members) also plays an important role in this respect. Indeed, correlations between the cultivated areas of the Botukebo village households and the number of adult females belonging to the households shows a high correlation (0.8). Similar correlations between the garden areas and the adult male population of the same households register only 0.29. Combining the sex with the marital status of the populations of individual households gives the following indices: for married women 0.64, for married males 0.58, for unmarried females 0.43. In contrast to these results, the number of unmarried males and the size of the cultivated areas show a negative correlation of −0.3. These results may suggest that it is the Kapauku female who actually accomplishes most of the cultivation, but a calculation of time spent by the two sexes on agricultural work shows that both men and women share about equally in this task. The reason why women exercise an important influence on the scope of cultivation does not lie simply in the amount of work they do. Because a woman has had to be paid for in the form of a bride price, she is regarded by the Kapauku as a financial investment. Consequently, the economically minded Kapauku feels that his investment must be fully exploited by providing the woman with enough work. However this does not mean assigning her certain tasks that she can do independently of the men. In the Kapauku agriculture the work of the sexes is interdependent. For example, women cannot weed and harvest unless the men have cleared and drained the ground and built the fences. Consequently, the women, and especially the married women, do not only work themselves but, more significantly, make the males work harder. The more women, especially married ones, there are in a household, the more the married men have to work in order to enable the women to be fully occupied. Kapauku marriage generally means that the female works harder than she did before her wedding, but it also transforms a carefree male into a diligent husband.

ANIMAL HUSBANDRY   In the Kapauku society the domesticated pig plays a role which is as important as that of the cow in the East African cattle area. The dark-skinned, long-snouted animal, whose body is covered with abundant bristles, represents not only an important source of proteins in the native diet, but its successful breeding and sale constitute the most important source of individual wealth and prestige. The pig functions as an indispensable part of the bride price, as a means toward achieving political power and position of legal authority, and it forms, together with the cultivation of sweet potatoes and the circulation of the cowrie shell money, the basis of the native economy. Around the mass slaughter of these animals the Kapauku have evolved large social ceremonies such as *juwo*, the pig feast, *tapa*, the fund-raising ceremony, and *dedomai*, the pig market.

The Kapauku pig is a fully domesticated animal. When it is about six weeks old the piglet is taken away from the sow and is entrusted to the care of a woman. She feeds the small animal with chewed, cooked sweet potatoes, and keeps it overnight in her quarters. When it is older, the piglet is taken to the old garden lands and swamps and is taught how to dig for roots, tubers, and grubs. In this way the woman keeper becomes a mother substitute for the animal, which follows her like a dog wherever she walks. When it is tired the woman puts it into her net carrying bag and carries it around like a baby. The pig becomes so attached to its keeper and her family, that when it is big enough to roam in the grasslands and forests and to sleep underneath the elevated floor of the Kapauku house there is little fear that it will become wild. The grown animals are fed sweet potatoes twice a day—early in the morning and at sunset. During the day they forage for themselves in the swamp, woods, and grasslands, augmenting the food they receive. Every pig is the exclusive property of a single man. The woman keeper is reimbursed by her husband with money or a piece of meat at the time of the pig's sale or slaughter.

Breeding and trading pigs is an activity which, if properly executed, may bring a Kapauku esteem from his neighbors, wealth, and the highest status in his society, namely that of *tonowi*, a rich man and a political leader. In order to achieve this highly desired goal a native must plan a production of pigs. The necessary first step is to plant sweet potatoes. After this, the young Papuan entrepreneur has to buy a pig, preferably a sow. He may save money for this purpose from payments received in the form of a bride price for his sister, or he may earn it by performing agricultural work and other services for well-to-do individuals. Often, however, he has to borrow this sum from one of his rich patrilineal kinsmen. If he succeeds in acquiring a female piglet he raises it and breeds it. When the litter is born he sells all the male pigs and preferably saves all the female piglets for breeding purposes. The increased stock requires more food, however, and the young man has to make more gardens in order to cultivate more sweet potatoes. He can easily accomplish this task himself or with the help of hired labor. Unfortunately it is not enough only to clear more land and to fence it in; the growing crops have to be weeded and harvested and the pigs have to be cared for and fed twice a day. Since all this is a woman's work the obvious course is for the young man to buy himself a wife. In this way the basic economic cycle of an increase in Kapauku production is completed. Ideally, it may be repeated as long as one has women to marry and luck with pig breeding: the more crops one grows, the more pigs can be produced, through whose sale one acquires money for the purchase of additional wives. Practically, however, this economic cycle cannot be continued indefinitely. Since a Kapauku wife is not a chattel, but a human being with a high degree of personal freedom and independence, she makes certain social demands on her husband. Because he is only human, he cannot meet these increased personal duties indefinitely. Consequently, there is a limit to the number of wives he can take. An extreme in this respect was achieved by Awiitigaaj, a rich headman of the village of Botukebo, who married ten native women and in 1959 contemplated marrying the eleventh.

In order to enable a native entrepreneur to keep as many pigs as he desires without having to marry a great many women, the Kapauku designed *ekina munii*, a pig-breeding contract. According to this agreement a custodian agrees to feed and bring up the animal until it reaches about 90 kilograms of weight. For this service the owner rewards him with about 6 kilograms of pork, the head and the intestines of the butchered animal, or with seven old Kapauku cowries. If a custodian brings up a sow, which later gives birth to a healthy litter of piglets, he is entitled to collect as high a reward as 20 old Kapauku cowries or one piglet from the litter. The burden of the risk of bringing up the pig entrusted to the custodian always rests with its owner. An exception to this rule is the custodian's gross negligence or intentional harm done to the pig. In such an event he is responsible for the damage done to the animal and has to pay adequate damages. This contract, then, allows rich people like Ijaaj Jokagaibo of Aigii to own as many as a hundred pigs without establishing a large and expensive "harem."

In addition to pigs the chicken is the only other domesticated animal kept by the inhabitants of the Kamu Valley. The Papuan dog, which is so important in the neighboring Kapauku regions of Mapia and Pona, is absent from this valley. The Kamu people have no reason for keeping this animal because of the scarcity of large game and the resulting unimportance of hunting. The poultry, which spread into the valley after having been introduced by the Dutch Administration in the Paniai and Tigi lake regions, found a good reception among the natives. They keep it for its meat and feathers rather than for the eggs. The birds, which are owned by single men in the same way as pigs, are fed broken pieces of sweet potatoes twice a day. In order to protect their domesticated birds against the elements and birds of prey, the Kapauku build them small chicken houses of reed and bamboo. In 1955, due to the recent introduction of the bird, the role of the chicken in the native economy was still negligible; seven years later it was becoming well integrated into the native culture. It was already being used as a substitute for rats and marsupials at ceremonies such as that celebrating the birth of a child.

HUNTING AND TRAPPING   The Kamu Valley is densely populated, and most of the larger game has been eliminated from the region by cutting down the low-lying sections of the forests. Nowadays when a man wants to bag a wild boar, cassowary bird, or large marsupials he has to walk several hours to the distant virgin forests where, with bow and arrows or by means of several types of traps, he still can secure some of this valued game. A wild boar may be stalked by a group of men. They follow its spoor and one of them, who has circled ahead of the others, shoots the boar from an ambush into which it has been driven by the rest of the hunting party. In regions where dogs are kept, their owners use them for tracking and engaging the boar until the hunters come close enough to kill the animal. There are also individuals among the Kapauku brave enough to seize a wild boar with their bare hands and hold it until a helper shoots or clubs the beast to death. The natives have designed several interesting traps for boar. One of these is a large, simple snare made of rattan. Another is a spiked spring designed to tear into the animal's abdomen. A large pit may also be dug on a trail that a boar uses regularly, the surface carefully camouflaged with branches and reed. Since there are no spikes in such a pit, the boar is caught alive and is subsequently shot with an arrow. A trapper may also exploit the boar's habit of raiding the native gardens: the fence of a sweet potato garden is lowered to lure the unsuspecting animal into jumping over the barrier, only to be transfixed by bamboo spikes hidden on the other side.

Other animals are either shot with an arrow on sight, hunted during moonlight expeditions, or trapped in snares. The small rats, which are abundant in the Kamu Valley, are subject to intensive hunting and trapping. They are either shot on their trails with four- or five-pronged hardwood arrows as they try to escape from a grassy area surrounded by male hunters and stamped over by the women, or they are trapped in numerous small snares set at the openings of their dens or on their trails.

The stalking method of hunting is also used on large birds such as a cassowary, mud hen, ducks, hawks, and herons. The hunter tries to approach the feeding or roosting target and discharge his hardwood or bamboo-tipped arrow from as close range as possible. Small birds, which are still abundant in the Kamu Valley, are shot with pronged or blunt-pointed arrows. The hunter either steals near to the roosting game and kills it from close range or he shoots it in the swamp from a specially designed dome-shaped hut. On dry and windy days a large group of natives may organize a communal hunt in the valley by starting an extensive grass fire and, while following the fireline, they simply pick up the roasted animals and birds. Of all the types of hunting and trapping only those that apply to rats and small birds are of any economic significance in the Kamu Valley.

FISHING   The Kapauku territory is dotted with numerous lakes and is drained by many streams and several large rivers. Of this water system the most spectacular features are three immense lakes, named after their discoverer, Wissel. They are located, north-to-south, in three large valleys, and are called Paniai, Tage, and Tigi. The huge Kamu Valley with its deep, sedimentary, flat swampy floor was also once a lake. Nowadays all that remains of this ancient reservoir are numerous small lakes and extensive swamps. Except for an economically unimportant and relatively rare species (*Oxyeleotis* sp.) all these waters are devoid of fish. To compensate for this deficiency the lakes and streams supply quantities of crayfish, water bugs, tadpoles, and dragonfly larvae, which are netted mostly by the native women. Equipped with large oval or small circular nets, they fish daily in the swamps and shallow waters, or use their nets in deeper water from a dugout canoe, in order to catch crayfish, amphibians, and insects in quantities large enough to provide a constant supply of these valued protein foods for their male relatives and children. The nets are used as scoops, or they are provided with long handles fastened to their oval frames and are dragged on the floor of the shallow lakes by the women who stand in their canoes. In deep waters the large oval nets are baited with pieces of snake, lizard, or sweet potato, weighted with stones, and sunk to the bottom. After a while they are pulled up with the crayfish that cling to the bait. The women also build a dam of reeds or stones across a stream and catch their prey in nets at an opening left in the center of the structure. The catch is inserted into tubular bamboo containers, which are plugged with a bunch of grass or leaves and are tucked under the belts of the fisherwomen. In addition to the nets the Kapauku women have devised another relatively easy way of securing aquatic organisms. Standing in their canoes they plunge long forked poles into the weeds of the lake bed, and by rotating them in their hands they uproot bundles of water vegetation. Then they pull the bundles up and spread them over the sides of the canoe where they can easily pick out the animals that hide in the weeds.

Men contribute relatively little to the fishing endeavors of the Kapauku people. Rather as a sport they dive to the bottom of the rivers and lakes and, holding to stones and roots they locate the crayfish and seize them by hand. Sometimes at night the men go to the lakes and rivers in order to lure the crayfish with torches and spear them with long, seven-pronged fishing spears.

Fishing rights in small, nonnavigable streams are owned in common by members of sublineages through whose territory they flow. Small lakes, on the contrary, are regarded as the property of the whole local lineage. Although they are legally considered to belong to the lineage members only, they are accessible for fishing to all members of the political confederacy to which the local lineage belongs. The navigable rivers and large lakes are regarded in a sense as "international"; they are free to everyone for navigation and fishing.

GATHERING   This activity is an indispensable part of the Kapauku economy. It provides the natives not only with important ingredients of their daily diet, but also with raw material for construction and manufacturing. Most of the collecting is done daily, but there are occasions in the Kamu Valley when gathering becomes a large-scale, organized activity. When a heavy rain transforms the Edege River into a surging torrent that spills over its banks and inundates the whole valley, changing it into a huge lake, the Kapauku women go out in their canoes to collect the insects that float helplessly on the water. Wherever there is higher ground where reeds and grass protrude from the water, the women stamp down the vegetation in order to force the numerous mole crickets, grasshoppers, stink bugs, cockroaches, and other species of edible insects into the water where they are easily caught. The catch is placed in sections of bamboo carried by the women underneath their belts. In the evening the filled containers are simply pushed into hot ashes and the contents are steamed in their juices for about thirty minutes.

Collecting insects, however, is by no means limited to the times of flood.

Gathering on a small scale takes place almost daily. On their way to their gardens or neighboring villages the Kapauku stop at various trees, shrubs, and rotten logs to inspect them for a possible stink bug, beetle, or grub. Occasionally they also find birds' eggs, an edible large lizard, a wasp nest with its delicious larvae, or a few mushrooms.

Frogs are systematically collected during a night expedition by a small group of women who blind the amphibians with light from torches, catch them with a small scoop net, and deposit them in bamboo containers. Frogs are caught regularly, and the Kapauku households derive from them an important supply of animal protein.

Kapauku also gather edible plants. Several species of wild greens are collected and steamed in pandanus-leaf bundles over low fires. Whenever a Kapauku has to prepare a large quantity of pork, he makes a steaming mound of pandanus leaves and reed, heated with hot stones. In this mound he steams his meat together with several varieties of fern that are regarded as the proper vegetable to be served with pork. Especially before pig feasts, *tapa* ceremonies, and pig markets the people make expeditions into the forests to collect these plants.

The Kapauku ideal rules state that collecting in gardens and secondary forests is an exclusive right of the members of the local sublineage, but the virgin forests and wastelands on the summits of the mountains and ridges are territories open to everyone for gathering. In actuality the Kapauku are much more lenient and do not supervise closely the gathering activities of those outside the local sublineage who collect edible plants and insects in the secondary forests. However, trespassing on the gardens under cultivation is a different matter. The natives suspect that any gathering of insects and wild plants in the gardens is only a pretense to allow thieves to help themselves to the cultivated crops and for this reason the rules on collecting and trespassing are strictly enforced on these premises.

Manufacture

As a contrast to the rather sophisticated agricultural methods, Kapauku technology and material culture appear to be among the simplest in the world. These Papuans live in a neolithic stage of development; their major tools are made of polished stones, wood, and bamboo. They know no metal, pottery, weaving, true basketry, sculpture, or painting. Their clothes are conspicuous for their scantiness. In only one part of their material culture do the Kapauku exhibit great skill and an artistic approach. Their complex and beautiful net carrying bags, made of inner-bark string, and decorated with the stem covering of colored orchids, are among the finest specimens of this kind that can be found in New Guinea.

SHELTER   Kapauku houses vary as to size, number of rooms, and some details of floor plan. However, all of them have many features in common and there is also what may be called a prototype of Kapauku house. Such a dwelling is about 6 meters long, 4.5 meters wide, and 4 meters high. It has an elevated floor (about 1 meter above the earth) that provides good insulation against the damp and often flooded ground, and furnishes quarters for the domesticated pigs. The walls are made of several layers of upright planks; the roof of the structure is gabled and thatched with either pandanus leaves or reed. The house is divided in half by a plank partition. This separates the *emaage*, the men's dormitory, from the rear half, which is composed of several *kugu* (small dormitories) for married women and their children. All the adolescent and adult males live and sleep in the common dormitory; each of the married women is entitled to her own room in which she lives with her children. Every room in a Kapauku house has its own fireplace, made of stones and sand (or mud), and has its own separate entrance from the outside. Sometimes two additional *kugu* are constructed in front of the men's dormitory, having between them a narrow, elevated passage into the men's quarters.

The Kapauku house is a well-insulated structure whose walls of several layers of planks also include screens of reed and an inside lining of pandanus bark. The floor is also covered with large sheets of the smooth bark that looks like linoleum. Most of the day and all during the night low fires for warmth burn in every room. The smoke from the fires rises slowly into the rafters and thatch and escapes through openings left between the plank walls and the roof.

In many large households the structure does not provide adequate quarters for all the married women. In this case the men build for their "surplus women" *tone*, a small rectangular structure of approximately 4 square meters of floor space, which usually stands only a few meters away from the main house. This small house has only one room with one fireplace, and provides shelter for one married woman and her children. In construction it is a small replica of the main house. The rich headmen, of course, with their numerous dependents cannot be satisfied with such an arrangement. Their houses are therefore usually much larger, with two additional rows of women's quarters on both sides of the men's dormitory and along the back half.

In addition to dwellings the Kapauku construct large feast and dance houses as a part of their preparation for *juwo*, the pig feast. These structures are described under ceremonies in the fifth chapter.

DRESS   As far as clothing is concerned, Kapauku care only for proper covering of their genitalia. The children of either sex up to six years of age wear simple small aprons in front and in back, composed of several strands of inner bark which are attached to a braided belt of the same material. After the age of seven, the boy covers his genitalia with a penis sheath made of an orange, tubular-shaped gourd. This is held in position by a braided belt, and is provided at its upper end with a stopper of marsupial skin that serves as a decoration. The adolescent girls wear a skirt that reaches to the knees and is made of loose strands of inner bark suspended from a belt. This garment looks like the famous South Seas grass skirt. When a woman menstruates for the first time she is expected to change her loose skirt for a sort of loin wrap which she will wear from that time on. This garment is basically a skirt similar to that described above, but with fewer, thicker strands of inner bark. It is worn in such a way that the strands are parted at the back, brought forward and passed between the thighs, and finally tucked in the back underneath the belt. There they hang down, resembling a crude apron.

In addition to these items of clothing the natives decorate their bodies with braided rattan armlets, bamboo earplugs, dog-, cuscus-tooth and shell necklaces, feather bonnets and hairpins, and various decorative net bags.

NETS   Well-netted decorative bags constitute the most conspicuous items of native manufacture. The Kapauku spin fine and cruder strings of inner bark of several species of trees and bushes. They employ these in three different netting techniques: *ginii*, consisting of simply interlocking "8 designs"; *pugi gou*, a complex 8 design achieved by interlocking each added 8 figure with two already completed 8s of the pattern; and *kupagine*, basically a simple coiling technique. These techniques serve the Kapauku for making utilitarian objects such as fishing nets and large carrying bags, as well as for the fine decorative bags. The purely utilitarian objects are usually made by the women; it is always the men who produce the artistic net bags. These decorative bags are often provided with boar tusks, cassowary bone spinners, or pendants of shell, pig tails, hawk claws, and feathers of the birds of paradise. They are often used purely as bodily decorations and are hung from straps either around the neck and left shoulder, or passed underneath the left arm, thus covering the left breast. Other smaller decorated bags are used as purses for shell money.

TOOLS   The basic Kapauku tools are made of stone, bamboo, or wood. For cutting down trees and making planks and canoes the natives use polished petaloid-shaped stone axes, which are oval in cross section. They are inserted into a perforated hardwood handle and held in position with a rattan lashing. Other stone tools include large lunar or straight stone knives, flint chips, and various sorts of grinding stones. Bamboo serves the Kapauku as water or insect containers. From its splinters they make bamboo knives which they use for carving pork or for surgical purposes. Wooden agricultural tools generally used are weeding, planting, and harvesting sticks, and large petaloid-shaped earth-knives for digging drainage ditches. A few surgical and carving tools are made of rat teeth and hawk claws.

WEAPONS   The Kapauku use bows and arrows, exclusively, for hunting. They do not make use of any close-combat arms, such as knives, clubs, or spears. Their bow, made of a simple hardwood or palm wood shaft, approximately 180 centimeters long and with a split rattan string, is a very effective weapon. It enables a good marksman to hit a man from a distance of even 60 meters. According to the various purposes, the natives use several types of arrows. All have shafts of reed and points of bamboo or hardwood. Exceptionally, an arrow may be tipped with a bird beak or bone. For hunting medium- and small-sized birds and rats the Kapauku use arrows with hardwood tips having several prongs. Small birds are usually shot with blunt-pointed arrows. Large game and human enemies are killed with single hard-wood-tipped projectiles, or with arrows that are tipped with long blades of bamboo. These latter missiles are regarded as very effective and are consequently very much feared as weapons of war.

The Kapauku Individualistic Money Economy

In Western society we are accustomed to think in terms of dichotomies and contrasts. The field of anthropology and economics has not escaped this tendency. We classify the various peoples of the world either as civilized or as primitive societies. While civilized people are popularly regarded as logical, having a complex technology, and an economy characterized by true money and by markets, primitive people have been credited with only a prelogical mentality, and a crude technology that has as its "logical" consequence a simple, nonmonetary type of economy. Their economy has been considered by various writers to be either overindividualistic or communistic. As will be apparent, the Kapauku society does not fit such oversimplified generalizations. It combines, strangely enough, one of the world's most primitive technologies with a rather sophisticated and complex economic system. The latter in its main features resembles a simplified version of capitalism rather than any sort of primitive communism.

MONEY AND MARKETS   Contrary to many generalizations about the nature of exchange in primitive societies, barter plays a minor role among the Kapauku. Despite their simple technology, sales (the acquisition of goods by money) are the regular means of exchange on the inter- as well as intratribal level; barter and gifts are always secondary to trade.

One of the major pillars on which the Kapauku economy stands is the use of true money. Cowrie shell and two types of necklaces function in this society as the common medium of exchange and the common measure of value. For this money one can buy not only food, domesticated animals, growing crops, land, and artifacts, but one can also use it as payment for labor in the gardens, for various services (such as surgery, magical curing, breeding of pigs), for the lease of land, and for damages and fines that originate from criminal as well as contractual delicts. Only money enables a man to get married, to gain prestige and become an influential individual, to conclude best-friendship unions with respected individuals, and to achieve the highest status of the political leadership and legal authority. Without money one is called *daba*—poor, idle, a not respected individual, who has no standing in the native society. The closest translation of this word is "tramp."

As in modern monetary systems the Kapauku cowrie shell money comes in various "denominations." The cheapest is a shell type called *kawane*, which is of eliptical shape with a smooth surface. Five such shells equal the value of one *tuanika mege*, a cowrie recently introduced from the coast that, except for its newness, has all the characteristics of a precious cowrie called *bomoje*. This valuable shell is the most frequent type of native money encountered in the Papuan trade. It has an angular outline and an uneven surface with occasional depressions and bumps. There are two types of these shells: *dege bomoje*, which is yellowish-white in color and is worth 15 *kawane*, and *buna bomoje* of darker, bluish or white color whose value is approximately 20 *kawane*. In addition the Kapauku have two other types of high-value shell: the *epaa mege* and the *bodija*. Both of these closely resemble the *bomoje* except that they are much larger. Whereas *epaa mege* is usually worth 2 *bomoje*, the value of *bodija* varies with its size. It is always valued more than *epaa mege*, and it may even reach the exchange rate of 10 or 12 *bomoje*. With the introduction of European glass beads of cylindrical shape and light blue color, the value of a Kapauku *bomoje* was set at 30 such beads in 1955. Besides the cowrie shell the natives also use as money necklaces of tiny cowrielike shells (*Nassarius* sp.) called *dedege*, and necklaces of small glass beads of various colors called *pagadau*. Both of these necklaces are standardized at the length of a human arm and are worth 1 *bomoje*.

Since none of the Kapauku shell money is produced by the people themselves, but has to be acquired through trade from the coastal lowland Papuans, the amount in circulation is limited. Indeed, the trade relations with the Kapauku lowlanders were, prior to the white man's pacification of the area, very irregular because of the dangers involved in this enterprise, since the lowland Papuans were not only keen traders but also expert headhunters and cannibals. Exchanges occasionally ended in unexpected ways, with the Kapauku traders themselves taken as a commodity for which no price was paid. Because of the uncertainties involved in this trade the coastal cowries have been always relatively scarce in the highlands and the demand for them great. It is my impression that prior to the contact with the white man the amount of cowries in circulation was almost static; the cowries lost, and through normal wear destroyed (split by the string), about equaled the import of these treasures. Thus the supply of old Kapauku money was about fixed and the value of the currency, determined by its scarcity, was generally stable.

MARKET AND PRICES   There are several interdependent factors in the price-making process. The relative scarcity of cowrie shell and long practice have established a scale of customary prices for commodities—that is, a set of ideals to which the actually charged prices "ought to conform." These customary prices are regarded by the people as ethically justifiable and fair, and the man who demands them is considered honest. There is seldom a dispute after a customary price has been charged and paid. When people are asked in general about prices of various commodites they always cite these ideals. Accordingly, the people quote 5 *bomoje* shell as the price for 900 square meters of land or for a crop growing on the same area. Lease of the same land costs 1 *bomoje*. A piece of pork of about 2 kilograms should sell for 1 *bomoje*; an introduced steel ax costs 5 *bomoje* and a steel machete 3 *bomoje*. A male pig of approximately 90 kilograms' weight which is destined for slaughter sells for 20 *bomoje*; seven large marsupials should cost 2 *bomoje*, and the customary price for 30 rats is 1 *bomoje*, and so on. However, the actual prices charged on specific occasions may, and often actually do, differ from the quoted ideals. Lacking an authority or a binding custom that could determine and fix the value of certain commodities, the Kapauku market relies heavily upon free and automatic adjustment of prices to the supply and demand. But this does not mean that the idea of a customary price would have no effect upon the actual price; indeed, it still remains an ideal. To pay the customary price means security for both parties to the contract. Sales of land especially conform to the ideal because if a price lower than customary has been charged for a plot of land, the seller or his heirs can always ask for the difference under the threat of repossessing the land after repayment of what they originally received.

Sales of other commodities are usually heavily influenced by the law of supply and demand. Although payment of a customary price also provides security here, since these goods, unlike land, are perishable, the security is not so desirable. This is especially so because Kapauku law guarantees no annulment of contract in case a lower than customary price has been charged for such commodities. Also, any security obtained from conforming to the ideal is almost always obtained at the expense of a greater financial profit to one of the parties of the sale. As consequence the ideals are frequently disregarded, and for the Kapauku market it is generally true that the higher the supply the lower the prices, and vice versa. The fluctuation of prices on the native market may often be so considerable as to dwarf the elasticity of prices in the Western economic system. For example, in February 1955 at a pig feast in Egebutu 2-kilogram pieces of pork were being sold for 2 *bomoje,* in other words for 100 percent more than the customary price. At another time there was such a high demand for pigs in the Kamu Valley that Ijaaj Amoje of Aigii suceeded in selling a pig, customarily worth 12 *bomoje* shell, for a price three times as high. On the other hand prices may fall well below the customary ones. In 1953 Pigome Ipouga of Obajbegaa, capitalizing on a large supply of pork, brought from Pigome Gaajabii of the same village 4 kilograms of pork for only 1 *bomoje,* which is exactly one half of the customary price.

In addition to the force of the ideal customary price and the law of supply and demand, the prices on the Kapauku market are influenced to some degree by particular relationships between the trading partners, by the force of competition, and by the status of the buyer. Often, but not as a rule, prices tend to be lower if the parties to the sale are close relatives. Also, prices charged between best friends, and between a debtor and a creditor may disregard to some extent the law of supply and demand. However, such a disregard is an exception rather than a regular occurrence when one takes into consideration the Kapauku market as a whole. More frequently the prices are depressed below the customary level by a competition among several vendors of the same type of commodity who are eager to sell, even if it means a loss with regard to the customary value of the merchandise. The status of the buyer may also influence the prices of commodities that he buys. A rich man or a political leader is especially likely to be offered "bargains" either because the seller expects future favors or because he feels grateful for past financial or legal aid.

Marketing of the Kapauku commodities takes place daily in an incon-spicuous, unceremonial way. However, the native "businessmen" do most of their selling and buying on special occasions of a ceremonial nature. There are three types of such occasions: *juwo,* the pig feast, *tapa,* the fund-gathering ceremony, and *dedomai,* the pig market. The pig feast is the most elaborate and conspicuous ceremony in the Kapauku culture. Its nature and structure, together with those of the other two ceremonies, are explained in some detail in the fifth chapter. Here we may limit ourselves to a few statements concerning its mar-keting function. Besides other important roles, such as entertainment, feasting, settling of political affairs, and dating, during its last day, called *juwo degii na-ago,* the Kapauku pig feast is a huge market. Often well over a 1000 sellers and buyers gather in order to offer their produce for sale or to make necessary purchases with their shell money. Usually hundreds of pigs are slaughtered dur-ing this day and the meat is distributed through sales, loans, and repayment of debts. The trading is, of course, not limited to pork and pigs. People offer for sale many other products of their labor such as salt, bamboo and gourd con-tainers, bundles of bowstrings made of rattan, packs of native tobacco, pandanus leaves for wrapping the native cigarettes, bows, arrows, net carrying bags, chick-ens, bundles of dried inner bark, axes, knives, and necklaces. Since a pig feast attracts people from faraway places, even from other Papuan tribes, this feast functions also as an important institution of interregional as well as inter-tribal trade.

The fund-gathering ceremony is far less conspicuous than the pig feast; its economic role dominates this event, while the social functions are only sec-ondary and often incidental. The major objective of the sponsors of this event is to gather funds through loans or collection of debts. In addition to these financial transactions the ceremony functions, like the pig feast as a large mar-ket. However, the volume of trade concluded at a *tapa* ceremony is far smaller than at a pig feast. The last of the ceremonies that supplies a market place for the Kapauku trade, *dedomai,* is the least ceremonial, its purpose being almost entirely economic. This occasion is devoted entirely to business. No dancing takes place and no ceremonial structures are erected. All people from the region as well as from other tribes are invited to participate in selling and buying the various produce. Since this event does not involve any conspicuous ceremonial processions, dances, or other performances, and because its only function is an in-formal redistribution of goods and shell money, *dedomai* may be regarded as a market place or a fair, and is comparable to the same institutions in the Western civilization.

EXCHANGE AND TRANSFER OF PROPERTY   Among the Kapauku an overwhelming amount of goods is exchanged through sales. Although Papuans do not discriminate against sale contracts concluded between strangers (which occur in large numbers at the markets just described), more sales are concluded within local patrilineal kin groups, and therefore between closely related people, than between complete strangers, because of their physical proximity. In their selling and buying most of the Kapauku are strictly profit motivated. Often they invest money in pigs, chickens, large *woti* (bailer shell), inner bark, or animal teeth, for the purpose of breeding the animals for profit, speculating in sales of the bailer shell, of for making artifacts for sale. In its emphasis on sales this primitive economy resembles the modern Western economic system. Besides the necessity of having to buy with money such commodities as land, manufactured products, labor, and services such as surgery, curing, and midwifery, the Kapauku have to pay for favors and acts for which even in our capitalistic society there is no charge. For example, one pays a bride price for a wife, the services of a foster father have to be paid for by the grown boy, a grief expressed by strangers or distantly related people over the death of a close relative has to be recompensed in money, and almost all crimes can be settled through a proper transfer of shell currency. The dominant position of sales in the native economy has pushed barter into an insignificant position. Barter, in addition, is provided with so many restrictions of a legal and traditional nature that it has become not only exceptional but also a means of exchange to be avoided if possible.

There is a major difference between the concept of the sale contract in Roman law and its counterpart in the Kapauku society. Among these natives a mutual agreement does not seal a sale. Not until the buyer receives the sold object and the seller his full payment does the transfer of ownership take place. Also a tacit underselling of nonreal property (less than the customary price), which is not accompanied by an explicit statement as to the finality of the transaction, allows the seller or his main heir to invalidate the deal at any time in the future. In other respects the Kapauku sale resembles our idea of this type of contract. Bargaining is acceptable, and the price and quality of the commodity are often hotly disputed. To almost every sale there are witnesses so that a possible future dispute can be adjudicated on the basis of objective evidence. Usually merchandise need not be advertised. It can simply be displayed at a market place or, if such a facility is not readily available, the news about a commodity for sale spreads by means of local gossip.

The Kapauku have designed many types of sale contracts to fit the various types of commodities; the contracts vary in their complexity according to the value of the merchandise. The sale of land is provided with several restrictions of a legal nature: if less than the customary price (5 *bomoje* for 900 square meters) is charged for the property, the sellers of the real estate, or his heirs, can at any time either annul the agreement or ask for the difference in price. An old man cannot sell his land validly without the consent of his sons; if he should do so, his heirs can always repossess the land against a return of the purchase price. Growing crops are also subject to sale. For a payment of 5 *bomoje* shell the buyer receives the right to harvest a crop of sweet potatoes on an area of about 900 square meters. The vendor is always responsible should the crop be damaged by weather or a pig; part of the price is returned, in proportion to the damage. Sale of a house is rather rare but involves a simple contract; the price varies with the size of the structure (from 3 to 5 *bomoje*), and the new owner is often expected to move the property to another site.

Since pigs are fundamental to the Kapauku culture, it is not surprising that their sale is elaborately regulated. There are basically two types of pig-selling contracts, one for a male pig, the other for a sow. A male piglet may be bought simply by paying the full price (6 to 7 *bomoje*) or by a down payment of 1 *bomoje* and a final payment (usually about 10 *bomoje*) at the time the animal is slaughtered. For an older pig one usually has to pay 1 *bomoje* shell for each 2-kilogram piece of pork that (it is estimated) can be cut from its carcass. In contrast to this simple transaction, selling a small sow is very complex. First, the buyer has to pay *bo badii*, a down payment that varies from 3 to 10 *bomoje,* at the time of purchase. Later, when the sow has had piglets and has been fattened, she is killed with some of her offspring. The buyer must then deliver to the seller a large payment called *epaawa,* which varies from 60 to 180 *bomoje.* The final payment for a sow is called *ijobai* and consists, according to the original agreement, of one or several female piglets of the sow. If, however, the sold female pig dies prematurely, the buyer is not only absolved from the subsequent payments, but he may actually request the return of the whole *bo badii* (down payment) against delivery of the carcass of the dead pig. Also, if the female pig proves to be sterile, the buyer is absolved from delivering the two subsequent payments. Thus the risk in the trade of a female pig rests on the shoulders of the seller.

Sales of chickens in many respects parallel those of pigs. Whereas a small rooster can usually be purchased for a simple payment of 1 *bomoje*, a hen is sold for a down payment of 1 *bomoje* and, if she lays eggs and hatches chicks, for an additional payment of 3 *bomoje*. As in the case of a sow, an *ijobai*, consisting of one or two female chicks, has to be paid later.

Of the various types of food sales, by far the most frequent are those of pieces of pork. The meat comes to the market in the form of *kado,* a piece of about 2 kilograms in weight and usually costs 1 *bomoje;* but the price, as has been already indicated, can vary greatly with supply and demand.

Next in importance in the trade of food comes salt. This mineral comes into the Kamu Valley through trade with neighboring regions, or special expeditions are undertaken by the inhabitants of the Kamu to the distant salt springs in the north (Moni country), where they themselves burn the leaves and wood soaked in the salt water and make "bundles of salt" from the ashes. The weight of these pieces of salt is about 2 kilograms each. The salt, which is stone hard and blackened from a high content of ashes, is wrapped in banana leaves and tied with rattan vine so as to form an elongated bundle that can be carried by a rattan strap. During an eight-month period in 1955 the 180 inhabitants of the village of Botukebo imported about 34.25 kilograms of salt. Except for 2 kilograms that were traded to outsiders, all the salt was locally consumed.

Game, especially rats and marsupials, is also traded between the natives. Because of the scarcity of wild life in the Kamu Valley, the region relies heavily on imports of roasted carcasses of these animals from the southern Pona Valley. For example, inhabitants of Botukebo village purchased from the outside, in 51 separate transactions, 160 rats and 38 marsupials in eight months in 1955.

The customary price for 30 rats is 1 *bomoje,* and for seven marsupials it is 2 *bomoje.*

Trade of raw material for the manufacture of artifacts, as well as of the finished products, is very active. Although influenced by the ideal "customary prices" the actual payments for bundles of inner bark, bowstrings, bamboo containers, fire saws, net bags, fishing nets, bows, arrows, axes, introduced machetes, and so forth are influenced by supply and demand. Thus a net carrying bag, whose price should be 1 *bomoje* shell is often sold for twice the amount when the supply of new products becomes low. There is one commodity that is deliberately bought for speculation; this is the large bailer shell, called by the natives *woti (Melo hunteri* Perry), supply and demand of which depends on irregular trade with the coast and therefore varies so remarkably in price from time to time, that the shell has become an article of great speculation among the natives. Many a wise Kapauku businessman buys a large quantity of these shells when their price is low and the supply high. He hides them (usually in one of the numerous holes and cavities in the limestone cliffs) until the price rises, when he may sell his shell for a profit as high as 200 percent.

The following figures represent the imports and exports for intervillage trade of the Botukebo community that occurred during an eight-month period in 1955. They sold their goods and services to outsiders for an amount equivalent to 6519 glass beads (or 317 *bomoje* shell, which may purchase double the amount of kilograms of pork); they expended 45,328 glass beads (or 1511 *bomoje* shell) on imports. As a result their balance of trade was strongly negative. The figures are somewhat distorted as the inhabitants of the village had a large pig feast in 1953 that left the livestock depleted although it brought lots of cash into the community. Because they planned another pig feast for 1957, during the eight-month period in 1955 they made disproportionately more purchases than would have been the case otherwise.

In their trading Kapauku do not limit themselves to partners of their own tribe. Indeed, the Kamu Valley constitutes but a segment in a chain of intertribal trade that starts in the south at the Mimika coast of New Guinea and continues through the Kapauku territory into the interior, at least as far as the Baliem Valley, or even farther. The whole intertribal trade resembles a chain reaction in which traders from many regions and tribes participate by exchanging their commodities, carrying the newly acquired ones for a relatively short distance and trading them again for other goods to their neighbors on the other side of their territory. In this way bailer shell, necklaces of the small *dedege* shell, iron axes, and machetes move along the route from the Mimika coast into the interior toward the northeast. From the northeast come red ochre, palm wood, stone axes, and stone knives. The stone tools, made of a fine serpentine and green jadeite, are manufactured by the Dani people. From the Moni Papuan country the southbound trade takes bundles of native salt as far as to the Mapia region of the Kapauku country. There, on the southern periphery of the Kapauku territory, all articles that arrive from the north are traded for dogs, net bags, and tobacco, which finally reach the Mimika coast of New Guinea.

In comparison to sales, barter in the Kapauku economy is far less important. For example, during the eight-month period in 1955 the value of bartered goods in the village of Botukebo amounted to only one tenth of the sales. However, if we include under sales any transaction by which one receives for money a commodity, a service, or a wife, then the volume of barter amounted to only 1 percent of the sales. Unlike sales, barter of various goods is subject to customary regulations that group the commodities into spheres of exchange. This means that only certain types of goods are mutually exchangeable. To exchange items belonging to two different spheres is not only improper, but appears to be legally invalid and is consequently not practiced. Needless to say, such rules necessarily restrict exchange through the channels of barter. The four spheres of exchange allow: (1) an exchange of pork for land, growing crops, steel axes, bows, net carrying bags, and salt; (2) bailer shell, bows, and net carrying bags to be bartered for growing crops and for pork; (3) a man to receive for his agricultural labor a reduction of the price to be paid for his wife, a free lease of land, or a growing crop; (4) artifacts, except canoes and planks, to be mutually exchanged.

In one respect the Kapauku distribution of goods appears more capitalistic than our own. The natives do not have the institution of gift, by which ownership of an item is transferred to a recipient who is not legally obligated to reciprocate with an equivalent value. In other words a Kapauku cannot forfeit, even by an explicit declaration, his legal right to request a return of something that has been given to another person. To a Kapauku the concept of *jegeka* means "a donation to be repaid in the distant future." If a "gift giving" occurs among good friends and relatives, "distant future" often means the lifetime of the donor or the recipient. Since debts are inherited, and an unreciprocated gift is regarded by a Kapauku as a debt, the repayment of gifts is promptly requested by the main heir as soon as the donor dies. In practice, repayment of a gift is usually asked at the time that the beneficiary acquires a substantial sum of money (from the sale of a pig, from a bride price paid for his sister and so on), or on the death of either the donor or the recipient. Although from the Kapauku legal point of view, little difference is made between debt and gift, the two concepts are not really identical. Whereas it is legal and moral to request repayment of a loan at any time, it is regarded as highly immoral to ask for a reciprocation of a gift shortly after it has been made. Consequently, Kapauku distinguish the concepts of loan and gift on the moral rather than legal plane.

As in our modern economy, Kapauku know the institutions of lease, rent, and loan. A plot of agricultural land of approximately 900 square meters is customarily leased for 1 cowrie. Lease of land for a monetary compensation is, however, not too frequent. Of all cultivated land of the residents of Botukebo (172,480 square meters) only 6.8 percent (11,800 square meters) was leased to their cultivators for a specific monetary compensation in 1955. Far more popular than leasing land for cash is to acquire it for cultivation as a "land grant in exchange." Kapauku refer to such a grant as *jegeka,* a gift. What is actually given is not the land, of course, but only the use of it, usually for one crop only. The natives request such grants because the plots they have in mind are bordered on one or several sides by gardens already made, thus saving the construction of fences and drainage ditches on those sides. Also, because of their promise of high fertility, plots that have lain fallow for a long time are in great demand. The land grant in exchange closely resembles a loan. In other words the recipient of the grant not only has an obligation to return the favor in kind, but the reciprocation of it is often requested within a short period of time. The grantee is required to return the "borrowed" land to its owner after he has harvested his crops from it. He is liable for all changes to the plot incurred by an improper use of it. In 1955 the cultivators of the village of Botukebo made about 34 percent of their gardens (57,900 square meters) on land obtained from others as grants in exchange. Movables, such as axes, adzes, machetes, and canoes are also loaned by their owners to others. If the borrower uses the tools for economic gain a small charge is invariably made for the loan. On the other hand, loans of necklaces and net carrying bags are free of any payment because they do not give a man any economic profit.

Extension of credit is another very important means of redistributing money among the Kapauku. It has greater importance in this society than in Western capitalism. Among the Kapauku the role of credit is not limited to the economic sphere only. Through a proper allocation of credit, which in itself is regarded by the Kapauku (who have no gift proper) as the highest expression of generosity and the safest way to acquire great prestige, a rich man assumes political leadership and also becomes a legal authority and judge in his group. The political and legal roles of credit will be fully treated in Chapter 3. The discussion here will be limited and will give the reader only one example of the importance of credit in the political sphere.

The Kapauku economy does not recognize the legal enforcement of interest on loan payments. Debtors often promise to pay a few extra shell for the favor of borrowing money, but this promise, if not kept, cannot become a cause for legal complaint. It is always entirely up to the debtor whether he will pay the extra sum; but if he refuses to do so, he faces a severe loss of prestige and will be regarded as an untrustworthy, dishonest individual. Ultimately this informal moral sanction carries with it economic repercussions; people hesitate to loan money to an individual who has broken his promise in the past.

The extent of credit may be illustrated by quantitative data on 170 cases of monetary loans involving 55 males as creditors or debtors. The total value of loans equaled 170,382 glass beads, an amount that could purchase 11,358 kilograms of pork. Fifty-one percent of all the loans were extended internally—that is within the village. External credits to outsiders accounted for 35 percent, and external debts amounted to the remaining 14 percent. The balance of external debts and credits proved to be favorable to the residents of Botukebo; the surplus of external credits equaled 66,379 glass beads, an amount capable of purchasing 4425 kilograms of pork. As for the relationship of the parties to these contracts, it was interesting to note that 46 percent of all cases of monetary loans were between paternal-parallel kinsmen.

The broad significance of credits can be described by demonstrating the consequences of an acculturation situation in the Kamu Valley that by severely reducing the amount of borrowing among the natives, profoundly changed the political structure of the region. Upon my second return to the Kamu Valley in 1962 a spectacular loss of power and influence of most of the native headmen was observed. Strangely enough, however, the Dutch Administration had shown a deep interest in preserving the old system of political leadership. A review of the outstanding debts and credits in 1962, compared with those of 1959 and 1955, explained the loss of power of the local headmen. Most Kapauku follow the decisions of the local headmen because they are indebted to them and are afraid of being asked to repay what they owe (explained fully in Chapter 3), because they feel grateful for past loans, or because they expect some future monetary favors. Comparison of the total of credits in the three years revealed that in 1962 the natives owed their rich headmen only about one fourth of what they did in 1955. It was therefore obvious that the disintegration of the headmen's power and, ultimately, the complete collapse of their leadership resulted from the spectacular decrease of indebtedness of the common native to his leader. The young men, who in former times had to borrow heavily from the headman in order to buy themselves wives or pigs, found, with the advent of the white man, a way to escape indebtedness. They secured remunerative employment at Moanemani, a government outpost where the Administration was building an airstrip. This construction had an unexpected effect upon the native Kapauku culture: by eliminating the necessity to borrow it caused the native political structure to disintegrate.

Intestate as well as testamentary inheritance plays an important role in the Kapauku system of redistribution of property. In their regulations of intestate inheritance Kapauku distinguish three different situations that determine the allocation of property in absence of a testament. Accordingly, different rules apply to the distribution of property left by a man or by a woman; the rules are again modified if the main heir is a minor. To every inheritance there is a main heir who is identified by a combination of the principles of primogeniture and patriparallel descent. Thus it is first the eldest son of the deceased who is the main heir to the estate. In the absence of sons the eldest living brother is the heir; in the absence of brothers the eldest son of the eldest brother inherits. If no first fraternal nephews survive, the father of the deceased inherits. In the absence of the father, the father's eldest brother becomes the main heir. In his deficiency the title to the estate passes to the eldest son of the father's oldest brother, and so on. Consequently, the difference between the three inheritance situations does not lie in the fact that different people would be designated as main heirs. Indeed, in all three situations he is the same person. Rather it is the degree of inclusiveness of the main heir's siblings in sharing the estate that marks the difference.

When a man dies, his eldest son or in his absence another main heir has an exclusive right to inherit the following objects: bows and arrows, net carrying bags, necklaces, charm stones, the main house as well as *tone* (the woman's house), dogs, chickens, all cowrie shell money and glass beads, and all pigs. If during his life the deceased had imposed a taboo on himself not to use certain cowrie shell, glass beads, and bead and *dedege* shell necklaces, but to leave them intact as an inheritance for his sons, all these become the property of the main heir. However, the heir has a legal duty to distribute some portion of them among his siblings. If these currencies have been kept during the life of the deceased by his wives, the sons of every wife are entitled to shares of those cowries kept by their mothers. All land, salt, and stone and iron axes are divided among the main heir and his siblings on the basis of mutual agreement.

From a woman her eldest son (or in his absence her husband or another main heir) inherits her shell necklaces and her net carrying bags. Although glass beads and *dedege* shell necklaces become the property of the main heir, he has a duty to give a portion of them to his siblings. Iron and stone machetes and stone kinves should be distributed among the sons on the basis of common agreement. The eldest daughter inherits only her mother's fishing net and large net carrying bag. If the deceased woman had no daughters, these articles become the property of her eldest sister.

When the main heir is a minor, his older brother (or father if he is not a son of the deceased) becomes a trustee of the inheritance and guardian of the minor. The guardian has the duty to bring up the boy properly and to help him with a loan in the purchase of a wife. In return the guardian is later paid *mune,* a fee for bringing up the child. Upon his coming of age the boy receives his father's land and all the tabooed currency that the guardian had kept for him. Of other inherited money the boy receives only a part; the rest is kept by the guardian. The latter also becomes the owner of all pigs of the estate and has no duty to return any of the animals to the main heir. Tools, necklaces, and weapons are also taken by the guardian who may keep most of them as his own property.

Every Kapauku who feels that he is going to die soon has the moral duty to make an oral testament in the presence of several witnesses. Most of these declarations simply dispose of the property according to the rules of intestate inheritance. Nevertheless, an explicit statement about the disposal eliminates possible uncertainties and difficulties pertaining to the division of the estate. Some testaments, of course, differ markedly from the laws of intestate inheritance. In order to protect the interests of legal heirs who might be unjustly eliminated, Kapauku law sets up certain restrictions to the free testamentary dispositions of a dying man. It categorically states that no sons, brothers, fathers, or nephews can be deprived of their share of land under any circumstances. A son, however, may be denied money and pigs if he abused or insulted the testator without a serious reason or neglected him in disease or old age. In the absence of sons these restrictions apply to any other type of heir. Bows and arrows, necklaces, net carrying bags, and fishing nets can be willed freely without restrictions.

The last type of redistribution of property is that which occurs by forceful seizure. The Kapauku law states that a man's property may be seized against his will if he has failed or refused to meet his obligations originating from a contract or from a damage he has caused. A successful seizure of the liable person's property, which inevitably takes the form of capturing a pig, absolves the debtor from any further obligation irrespective of the value of the seized property. The natives usually resort to forceful seizure in cases that cannot be legally adjudicated. This happens when the debtor and creditor belong to two different political confederacies in which case no single legal system applies. As will be demonstrated later, in the Kapauku society law exists only within a political confederacy that forms, politically speaking, a completely independent unit. Beyond the boundaries of this group affairs are settled either through diplomatic negotiations or violence, which takes the form of forceful seizure or war.

ECONOMIC INDIVIDUALISM   These capitalistic features of the Kapauku economy, such as the existence of true money, savings, and speculation, a market regulated by the law of supply and demand, an emphasis on wealth that surpasses in its magnitude that encountered in our own society, the dominant position of sales in the exchange of commodities, the use of paid labor and of lease contracts, are combined with a strong indigenous version of individualism. This manifests itself especially in the Kapauku system of ownership. Every material item that the natives possess is owned individually, a common ownership being simply inconceivable. They claim that two men cannot own a plot of land together because they would try to exploit each other by stealing from each other's crops and by avoiding work as much as possible. Thus money, movables, canoes, houses, and land have always only one owner. Even tracts of virgin forest belong to individual Kapauku. There is no common porperty of a group such as a lineage, village, or family. Even large structures erected for the benefit of a whole village are not, strictly speaking, owned by the residents in common. A main drainage ditch, or a large fence that protects an area consisting of gardens of numerous owners is, legally speaking, composed of many segments owned by specific individuals who care for the upkeep of only their particular property. Even a bridge across a river does not belong to a village as a whole. This becomes obvious if the structure collapses or if, for any reason, it has to be taken apart. Individuals who have built the structure come to claim the logs and poles that they contributed to its construction. Wife and husband also possess separate property, as does even a boy only twelve years old. It is a frequent occurrence that spouses or father and son are indebted to each other and that debts are payable upon request.

The notion of individualism and a relative financial independence are inculcated into the Papuans at a very early age. When a boy is about ten years old his father gives him a garden plot and encourages him to work on it for his own benefit. The boy gradually develops its production and begins his own financial career. He often plays the role of creditor or debtor to his father, older brother, or cousin. I was once a witness to a very interesting and amusing lesson on individualism that a young boy received from his father. While walking through the village of Botukebo I heard a loud howling and lamentation coming from one of the houses. When I entered the structure I found to my surprise a middle-aged, muscular man squatting in the middle of the room, crying and yelling while a boy, about eleven years old, was screaming at him and hitting him with a stick. The man was being beaten by his own son. The reason for the excitement was that the father owed his son 2 *bomoje* shell which he refused to pay back. Thus the boy had a right to punish his debtor. However, by the beating he abrogated his right to the debt, in other words the father's obligation to repay was annulled. After the beating was over and the enraged boy departed, the father wiped away his tears and smiled with great satisfaction: "My boy will be quite a businessman, but he must learn not to trust anybody." In addition to the lesson in commerce the whole affair proved to be most satisfactory to the happy father, as he assured me. Not only had he gained 2 cowries, but the beating administered by his son, he insisted, was so painless that he received the wealth for practically nothing.

Native individualism also affects the cooperation in a household, as well as the pattern of work in general. The people do not like to, and actually do not, work together on the same plot of land. Co-wives, for example, will never till land as a group; a plot is subdivided into *medeke,* individual sections, which are then entrusted to the care of individual women. Men also make gardens individually. If a helper is required in order to clear a large tract of forest, the area is invariably subdivided and each man works in his own section alone. Kapauku firmly believe that an individual should be free to make his own decisions and organize his work according to his own wishes.

Even eating does not escape this pronounced individualism. Unlike many primitive societies, Kapauku, in a strict sense, do not share their food in common in any social group. There are always individuals who own the food and function as hosts to the rest of the household. Those men who were treated to a meal by one of their coresidents have a duty to reciprocate in kind, and they are hosts in turn. Since women eat separately in their small rooms they do not participate directly in this distribution. The food that is customarily harvested by the men they receive from their husbands. They reciprocate these gifts of pork, game, sugar cane, bananas, and so on by supplying their spouses daily with sweet potatoes. In his work *Trade and Market in the Early Empires* (1957: 46) Polanyi generalizes for "tribal societies" and claims that a community "keeps all its members from starving unless it is itself borne down by catastrophe in which case interests are again threatened collectively, not individually." This theme of collectivism is certainly not applicable to the Kapauku situation. Among these Papuans there exists no collective action that would keep individuals from starving. The individual differences in wealth and consumption of food are striking. The Kapauku individualism indeed permits the natives, particularly children from poor homes, to develop severe symptoms of undernourishment, while the residents of the neighboring prosperous households are well fed. The village of Botukebo may serve us again as an example. There, members of the household of the old Kamutaga certainly starved, while their neighbors from the house of Timaajjokainaago lived in plenty. This difference in the state of economic affairs was plainly visible in the physical appearance of the residents of the two households.

Cooperation, to be sure, does exist among the Kapauku, but its pure form, which de-emphasizes individualism, is limited to a few activities. Thus people work together when erecting a building either for habitation or for festivity, when they pull a canoe to a lake, or when they are fighting a war. In other events that require the joint effort of several people, their activity appears to be somehow autonomous. Although several persons may work on the same project, their tasks are so defined that the contribution of an individual is readily perceivable and separable from that of others. In this way the work is either easily remunerable, or the fruits of the cooperation are retained by the workers.

Although the Kapauku economic system resembles in so many ways Western capitalism, there exists one important difference. The system is not combined with the sociological phenomenon that Veblen calls conspicuous consumption. In contrast to our own civilization, the rich men among the Kapauku dress as the commoners do. If they have some special food they tend to be secretive about its consumption, so as to avoid a possible sharing with others. Very often rich men's elaborate necklaces are loaned to the poorer people to wear, while the owners remain undecorated. Kapauku, of course, display their wealth, but through the channels of conspicuous generosity. Since these people do not know the gift proper, generosity may take the form of loans, or lavish distribution of food free of charge on such occasions as birth ceremonies or *putu duwai naago,* the opening day of the cycle of dances connected with a pig feast. There exists almost a compulsion for extension of credit in this native society. In some regions, such as that of the Paniai Lake, rich people who prove to be stingy with their credits are even punished by execution.

The wealth of a native, and therefore also his prestige and political status, changes with his successes and losses in pig breeding and trading. Consequently, the economic as well as the political structure is constantly undergoing change. New and successful pig breeders are elevated to the position of *tonowi,* the rich headmen, only to lose their positions later to younger and more successful businessmen. More so than in Western society the rich men among the Kapauku are self-made, thus testifying to the great vertical mobility in their economic and social system.

2

Social Organization

W HEN ONE ASSUMES a structural approach in the investigation of the organization of a society it is important to the analysis to distinguish two types of relationships: Ego's relation to the rest of the members of his society, and the structure of relationships of the various segments of the society. From the structural point of view these two types of relationships are basically different. In the first, Ego is always the common point of reference and the relationships are always described and defined *relatively* with respect to Ego. If these relationships pertain to aggregates of people who behave vis-à-vis Ego in the same or a similar way or in a concerted action, then such aggregates (having only Ego as a common link) do not constitute absolute units within the matrix of the society. They are relative entities that do not merit being called groups. To such an analysis of Ego's relation to the rest of the members of his society I propose to apply the term "social structure."

The second type of relationship does not utilize Ego as a central point of reference. Indeed, the analytical approach here starts with the society as a whole, and the investigation focuses upon the nature of the relationships of the society's *absolute* segments (subgroups). In the context of this analytical approach, which I propose to call the analysis of "societal structure," the aggregates of people that are investigated are absolute social entities constituting true social groups. Membership of individuals in such segments (groups) ia absolute; it does not necessitate (as a contrast to the situation in the social structure) a special relationship of each of the members to a referential Ego. While the memberships of the aggregates of social structure endlessly overlap in accordance with the shifting reference to the various Egos, the groups of the societal structure are mutually exclusive, their membership being defined absolutely and independently upon any particulat Ego. Whereas in social structure the inquiry concerns Ego and his relations to the members of his society, in societal structure the investigation follows an opposite direction, taking the society as a whole as its starting and referential point, and proceeds with the investigation of the patterned relationships of its discrete, absolute segments—the social groups.

Social Structure

From the point of view of a Kapauku Ego those members of his society with whom he has social relations belong to two types of aggregates: social categories and social quasi-groups. In both cases the structure of the relationships within the aggregates takes Ego as a point of reference. The individual members of the aggregates have mutually independent relations with the common Ego. Consequently, the members themselves may not be mutually related at all. Furthermore, since every social category or quasi-group is relative by being Ego-oriented, every individual within the society possesses a distinct set of these social aggregates that are, of necessity, different from similar social aggregates of any other member of the society. There is, however, an exception to this rule in the kinship structure, full siblings share categories and quasi-groups of consanguineal kinsmen. The two types of social aggregates exhibit an important difference that is suggested by the terms "categories" and "quasi-groups." The social categories are classes of individuals whose relationship and behavior toward Ego are defined in the same way, but in their behavior vis-à-vis Ego these individuals act, as a rule, independently of each other. Members of a quasi-group, however, whose relationships toward Ego are also patterned along the same lines, do not necessarily behave independently, but unite themselves from time to time into temporary groupings while pursuing an activity on behalf of Ego.

SOCIAL CATEGORIES   From Ego's point of view the Kapauku classify all people into three broad categories: *imee bagee*, close friends and kinsmen (lit.: "the pertinent kind"); *ojaa bagee*, acquaintances and strangers (lit.: "the not pertinent kind"); and *jape bagee*, a traditional enemy (lit.: "the enemy kind").

Imee bagee consist of 23 categories of relatives, some of whom Ego acquires by birth (consanguineal relatives), and others through the institution of marriage (affinal relatives). Each of the 23 categories is provided with distinctive kinship terms, and the behavior of the members of each category vis-à vis Ego (and vice versa) is defined by a special pattern of rules. These pertain, for example, to the kind of joking, power relations, legal liability, duty of blood vengeance, economic dependence, duty to participate in various ceremonies, obligation to contribute to certain payments, degree of emotional involvement, and so forth. For detailed definitions and analysis of the kinship categories the reader is referred to my article "The Kapauku Papuans and Their Kinship Organization" (Pospisil, 1960). Ego's close or "best friend," *maagodo noogei*, is equated with brother, and kinship terms and pertinent behavior are extended to his primary relatives. Kinsmen and best friends are the only people a Kapauku

trusts and is fond of. He relies heavily upon their financial, economic, and political support, which often are unsolicited.

The category of *ojaa bagee* includes Ego's acquaintances as well as complete strangers and foreigners. This comprises a mass of people with whom a
Kapauku has casual social or trade relations. Since every stranger is a prospective
customer, and thus a means of furthering the individual's wealth, Kapauku are
not unduly suspicious of, and are very seldom hostile to strangers. They certainly
do not regard them as personal enemies unless, of course, the stranger invites
such a status by his behavior.

Jape, the enemy, are a very special category of people who assume this
status in relation to Ego by ascription rather than by any hostile actions on their
part. *Jape* are not necessarily Ego's personal enemies. They are defined by
tradition, by the fact of their membership and Ego's in particular political
groups. A Kapauku's enemies are members of a traditionally hostile political
confederacy (or confederacies) who have periodically waged war against the
political groups of his father or of his residence. Since Ego classifies as his *jape*
not only the traditional enemies of his father's political confederacy, but also
those of his foster father, best friend, and of the group of his actual residence
(which is not necessarily that of his father), a *jape* category is different, in its
totality, for almost every Ego in the Kapauku society.

SOCIAL QUASI-GROUPS   In Kapauku social quasi-groups (that is, aggregates of people whose members have a special relationship to a common Ego and
who form temporary unions while acting on his behalf) the kind of unified effort and activity is defined by custom, and the occurrence of the joint action is
determined by the nature of the common activity. Accordingly, the consanguineal relatives, for example, who are expected to help Ego in an armed conflict or to contribute to the *kade* portion of the bride price paid for his wife
unite on the occasion of a war that involves Ego's confederacy or on the day of
his payment of the *kade,* in order to support their common relative by fighting
for him or helping him pay his monetary obligation. In a similar way, the affinal
relatives come together on the occasion of a *tapa* ceremony sponsored by Ego in
order to contribute loans to the *dabe uwo* (a reward given by Ego to the avenger
of the death of one of his close relatives).

In their relationship and activity toward Ego the consanguineal relatives, referred to as *okai ma bagee,* form a quasi-group that accords, strange as
it may seem, the definition of kindred. It is Ego oriented, bilaterally extended,
and possesses several important functions. Like a kindred of a bilateral society,
this Kapauku quasi-group is collaterally as well as vertically limited. In their
recognition of true blood relationship the Kapauku go as far as fourth cousins
in the collateral dimension, and as far as the fourth ascending and descending
generations in the vertical dimension. Because such aggregates of consanguineal
relatives are true quasi-groups, they overlap endlessly and every Ego in the society (except full siblings) possesses one of his own. All Ego's consanguineal
relatives are assigned proper kinship terms, share with Ego a mutual duty of

blood vengeance and payment of *dabe uwo* ("the blood reward") and are expected to participate in a mutual general assistance in financial matters. They are especially required to contribute to the *kade* part of the price paid for Ego's bride. In their attendance at Ego's birth ceremony, Ego-sponsored fund-raising ceremony (*tapa*), Ego's wedding (*kade makii naago*), and Ego's funeral, they unite into temporary groupings.

A subdivision of this grouping of consanguineal relatives is formed by paternal "parallel" kinsmen. They include all paternal consanguineal relatives with the exception of paternal cross-cousins, paternal cross-nephews (such as SiSo, SiDa, FaBrDaSo, male speaking; or BrSo, BrDa, FaBrSoSo, female speaking), and paternal cross-aunts (such as FaSi). Members of this quasi-group share with Ego a common legal responsibility for each other's crimes, a mutual duty of blood vengeance, and a reciprocal duty to pay *dabe uwo*, a reward to the man who avenges the death of either Ego or of one of the parallel kinsmen. In addition to these duties, Ego shares with every member of this quasi-group a reciprocal right to *me mege*, the blood money, paid by a killer of any of these individuals. In the profit-biased Kapauku culture the paternal parallel consanguineal relatives are especially important for their continuous and extensive financial and legal support rendered to Ego. Their financial aid becomes especially important at the time of Ego's marriage, when these relatives not only contribute to the *kade* but also to the *one* part of the bride price. Ego never feels ashamed to ask these relatives for financial aid.

The rest of the consanguineal relatives form another important quasi-group. They unite themselves particularly when Ego needs to be sheltered against the wrath of his parents who are supported by his patriparallel relatives of the previously described quasi-group. At such times they provide Ego with food, protection, and shelter, and their houses often function as asylums for a young fugitive from parental justice. Such protection is especially appreciated by a girl, who, after having refused to marry a man selected for her by her parents or brothers, wishes to hide until the anger of her family, and the eagerness and marriage lust of her suitor subside. In addition to the protective function, the relatives of this quasi-group share to a small degree with Ego the joint legal liability and the right to *me mege*, the blood money. They also assist him in payment of *dabe uwo*, the vengeance reward, and in daily financial matters; but these rights and duties are secondary to those of the paternal parallel relatives. Their only primary duty is to contribute to the *kade* part of the bride price; they are often excused from contributions to *one*, the main part of the marriage payment (for details see Chapter 4).

Another quasi-group, whose members' relations with Ego resemble in some instances those of the residual consanguineal relatives just described, are *baakaani*, the affinal kinsmen. There is no liability for crimes and debts, and no right to blood money. Their mutual financial assistance, however, approximates closely that rendered to Ego by the residual consanguineal relatives. On the other hand, the affinal relatives do not contribute to the bride price paid by Ego, neither do they support him in his marital troubles. If Ego sponsors a *tapa* ceremony (therefore is required to pay a reward for avenging the death of one of his relatives), the affines extend to him loans that must later be repaid.

Didee bagee is an interesting quasi-group comprising close consanguineal relatives of Ego; its membership cross cuts three of the preceding quasi-groups. Unlike these groupings, membership of this quasi-group is not determined purely on the basis of genealogical principles. Here no difference is made between paternal and maternal consanguineal relatives, nor has the degree of collaterality any relevance in this definition. The *didee bagee* are those consanguineal relatives of Ego to whose designation he can add the word *didee*. The word itself can be translated as "true, closest," or "not extended." Whenever a Kapauku adds *didee* to a word it simply means that he is referring to the genealogically closest kin type covered by the term. For example, *aneepa* signifies patriparallel cousins of any degree of collaterality. An *aneepa didee*, however, means his *first* patriparallel cousin; similarly, *naama didee* refers to MoBr or a male speaker's SiSo or SiDa. Thus *didee* designates the relatives closest to Ego and eliminates all those kinsmen that are called *naama epee*, who may be regarded as secondary to the *didee* kin types (such as MoMoSiSo; male's MoSiDaSo; male's MoSiDaDa). The quasi-group of *didee bagee* has a very important function pertaining to the regulation of marriage; it is exogamous. According to the Kapauku ideal, sexual intercourse or marriage between two persons designated as *didee* constitutes incest and should be punished by the death of both culprits. In addition, the *didee* relatives are tabooed from engaging in *ebaa mana* (lit.: "close talk"), flirtatious talk and joking. They function as a group on behalf of Ego in cases of crisis such as war, serious legal dispute, disease, or Ego's funeral.

A Kapauku usually calls one or several individuals *maagodo noogei*, his best friends. Since Ego's best friends form a quasi-group, they themselves need not to be mutual friends at all. Best friendship is characterized by frequent interaction of the friends, unconditional support in financial, legal, and political matters, and an extension of kinship terminology to the primary consanguineal relatives. A Kapauku's best friends function together as a group especially on those occasions that require gifts intended to alleviate his grief. Thus, for example, each of them is expected to present him with a pig when for the first time in his life he becomes so excited as to perform *wainai*, a mad dance, or when his close relative (father, child, or brother) dies.

As was pointed out in the previous chapter, the Kapauku cultural inventory does not possess the institution of a proper gift. As a consequence, extension of credit is regarded as a kind of high generosity. Because of this feeling and also because of the dependence of indebted persons upon their creditor, a man's debtors are regarded as among his best and most reliable political and legal supporters. By threat of withdrawing credit he can almost always gain their support. Since Kapauku do not lend money for determined periods of time, credits may be recalled at any time. In Ego's political and legal disputes as well as during his *tapa*, the fund-raising ceremony, the debtors, while supporting his arguments or paying back all or some of the loaned money, unite into temporary groupings.

MARRIAGE   The institution of marriage is a relationship that belongs to the social structure. Kapauku legal rules (such as those whose violation is regularly punished by the members of the society), incorporate only three principles that regulate marriages within the tribe. Two of these pertain to the social structure and one refers to the absolute groups of the societal structure. Stated briefly, a Kapauku is prohibited from marrying any relative who belongs either to his *didee bagee* (see the foregoing) or to a generation that is different from that of Ego. In addition to these restrictions he is also forbidden to marry a *keneka,* a sib mate (a societal principle). Offenders against these rules are to be punished by death, unless violation of the second principle (restricting marriageability to Ego's generation) occurs between Ego and an affinal relative further removed from Ego than two connecting links. In this case the juristic precepts are more lenient and only a beating with a stick is required. While marriage to all widows of affinal relatives is tabooed, widows of consanguineal relatives are Ego's potential spouses if they are not his sib mates, and if they were not married to Ego's consanguineal relatives of other than Ego's generation. Violation of the rules pertaining to marriage with widows is punished by death if the widow had been the wife of a relative connected with Ego by only two links or less. If, however, her late husband was Ego's more distant relative, only a stick beating should be the punishment for the culprits. The Kapauku tribe is a strictly endogamous group, the violation of endogamy being punished by death in the old days.

Since Kapauku law sets no further restrictions on marriage than these, polygyny as well as sororal polygyny, sororate, and levirate are permissible. General polygyny is regarded as the more desirable, more economical, and status-enhancing type of marriage, but the other three types are tolerated. Genealogies collected from several lineages reveal that approximately one third of all Kapauku marriages are polygynous.

Societal Structure

Unlike social structure that consists of the patterns of Ego's relations with the rest of the members of his society, societal structure refers to the structure of the society as a whole; that is, to the configuration and mutual relationship of its segments. These segments form discrete social groups with absolute, nonoverlapping memberships. In such social groups social relationships are not limited to those that emanate from a centrally referential Ego, as was the case in the quasi-groups, but they pertain equally to all the members, connecting each of them with everyone else.

TRADITIONAL UNILINEAL KINSHIP GROUPS   Groups of this first category of segments of Kapauku society determine their membership on the basis of patrilineal descent. These groups do not form residential units; their nonlocalized membership consists of individuals who belong to localized lineages which are scattered throughout the large Kapauku territory. Since members of these groups are unable to trace their actual relationships, they are recognized only traditionally. The dispersed settlements of the members prevent a political organization of these social segments. Their primary functions pertain mostly to marriage regulation, religion, and mythology.

The most important of the Kapauku traditional kinship groups is *tuma*, the sib. It is an ideally exogamous, named (for example Ijaaj, Pigome, Dou), totemic, patrilineal group, whose members believe that they are descended from a common ancestor. The native tradition claims that Ugatame, the Creator, founded all the sibs and determined that each of them should be mystically related to two or more animal or plant totemic species, which the members are forbidden to consume under the penalty of deafness. It is also asserted that the Creator prohibited marriages within a sib. Since violation of this incest taboo is believed not only to cause supernatural death of the culprits, but also to inflict general harm upon the whole sib membership, Kapauku law regards the violators as heinous criminals and punishes them by death. It is hoped that such an execution performed by the sib mates themselves will placate the Supernatural and thus avert calamity from the group.

Sib membership has an additional functional that pertains to intestate inheritance. One of the rules that regulates this type of transfer of chattels states that Ego's main intestate heir belong to his sib, no matter how distant he may be.

Two, and sometimes more sibs are grouped into loose unions that we may call phratries. Like a sib, a Kapauku phratry is a traditional, patrilineal kinship group, but it does not have a term in the native vocabulary, nor does it bear a proper name. A myth accounts for the relationship of the sibs that constitute a phratry. It explains how the junior sib originated from its senior partner. All members of a phratry share the same totemic taboos, which are identical with those of their sibs. In addition to the totemistic proscriptions, they also are forbidden to marry and wage war against members of another particular phratry. However, unlike the sib, a Kapauku phratry is not an exogamous group. Individuals are permitted to marry into the other sib of the same phratry. Since the common totemic taboos do not prevent such people from intermarrying, it is obvious that the Kapauku totemism is not related to their concept of incest.

Almost half the sibs whose members live in the Kamu Valley are further subdivided into moieties that we may call subsibs. Although there is no term for a subsib in the Kapauku language, each of these groups is referred to by a proper name that is added to that of the sib. For example, the Ijaaj sib consists of two subsibs: Dege-Ijaaj (lit.: "light warm-colored Ijaaj") and Buna-Ijaaj (lit.: "very dark warm-colored Ijaaj"). Although the members of two subsibs that belong to the same sib regard themselves as traditionally related, they always belong to different political confederacies and, as a rule, wage intermittent wars against each other. Consequently, killing a man of one's own sib, but of the other subsib, is regarded as a regrettable but often unavoidable necessity. No moral stigma or legal reprimand ensues from such action. In contrast, taking a life within one's own nonlocalized subsib (also not punished legally if the victim and the killer belong to different confederacies) is nevertheless regarded as murder, and the offender suffers from informal ostracism, gossip, and often from public insults. If such a killing carries serious political consequences, the culprit may even be extradited to the group of the victim for punishment. This may be either execution or payment of *me mege*, the blood money.

LOCALIZED UNILINEAL KINSHIP GROUPS   This category of kinship groups includes only two types: the lineage and the sublineage. Both of these groups are localized, their members occupying contiguous territories. Because of this localization and fission by which large sublineages become independent lineages, the population of these units is kept to a reasonably small number so that their members can accurately trace their mutual genealogical patrilineal relationship and refer to each other with proper kinship terms. Since residence in the group's territory is required for full membership, those individuals who for various reasons live in outside villages have only "latent membership." Only upon their return to their home group can they reactivate their full membership right. Because of their localization both lineages and sublineages are politically and legally organized groups, performing important functions in both of those fields.

Lineage is the largest localized kinship group in which all the members can trace their actual relationship through male ancestors to a common founder of this group. It is also the largest group of kinsmen that is politically and legally unified. Within this group law and order are maintained by the juristic practice and political and economic inducement of *tonowi*, the headman. Since a lineage as a rule is not a large enough group to be significant in warfare, several such groups unite themselves (by recognizing a unified leadership in war, diplomacy, and settling of interlineage disputes) into loose unions that I have called political confederacies. Thus lineages form discrete, semi-independent "social blocks" of which the Kapauku political structure is composed.

The larger lineages are often divided into sublineages whose members trace their common descent from the various sons of the founder of the lineage. Each sublineage has its own territory, which forms a segment of the geographical area occupied by the whole lineage. It is regarded by the members of the sublineage as their true home. Not only may they build houses and make gardens in any part of this territory (provided they have secured a proper title to the land), but none of the prohibitions against trespassing, lumbering, trapping in virgin forests, fishing in streams, and collecting of wild plants and insects (that affect the rest of the lineage members and outsiders) applies to them on this land. In their behavior members of the same sublineage exhibit mutual affection and a strong sense of belonging and unity. Any kind of friction within the group is regarded as deplorable, and it is the duty of the sublineage headman to settle peacefully the internal grievances as soon as possible. As a consequence of their close relationship, mutual support, and interest in each others' affairs, members of this group share a liability for each other's crimes

against outsiders. The injured outside party often directs his self-redress indis-
criminately againt the property of any of the sublineage members, irrespective
of the particular ownership rights.

Whereas the traditional unilineal kinship groups present a rather static
picture, the localized kinship groups undergo constant, although usually slow
change. Due to the numerical increase of the membership, adding of generations, and a loss of knowledge of common ancestry, the sublineages become
lineages and split apart from the originally united group. As time passes, the
newly created lineages with their increased membership segment again into
sublineages that, in time, will again undergo a fission process. This being true,
the question arises whether the endless process of segmentation and fission
does not result in minutely subdivided territory in which the lineages and sublineages have areas too small to support their ever-increasing populations. The
dynamic aspect of the Kapauku societal structure fails to have such a disastrous
effect upon landholding for several reasons. First, it is obvious that many localized groupings do not increase in this way. Famine, accidents, disease, and a de-
cline in the number of sons born block the increase and sometimes even cause
a slow decrease of the membership. When the number of males reaches a
certain minimum the group is almost sure to die out, and its territory will be
annexed by their more prolific neighbors. In the southern Kamu Valley the village of Obajbegaa is such a case. There the growing Pigome-Obaaj lineage is
slowly but surely replacing the rapidly dwindling population of the Ijaaj-Ni-
bakago sublineage, and with equal pace it is absorbing its territory. In one or
two generations this diminishing sublineage will vanish from the inventory of
the localized groups of the Kamu Valley. The dynamic process of the societal
change can, however, sometimes take an abrupt leap. Such is the case in wars
when male populations of lineages or sublineages are decimated, and it is only
a matter of time before the groups die out. For example, a prolonged war in
the southwestern part of the Kamu Valley virtually wiped out the male population of the village of Degeipige. Sib mates of the killed villagers, who belonged to neighboring sublineages, moved into the territory to take care of the
almost vacated land. Sometimes a whole sublineage "packs up," turns over its
territory to its sister sublineage, and departs for another "underdeveloped region." The Pigome-Obaaj lineage originated in this way; its people came to the
Kamu Valley from the Paniai Lake region. The founders of the Ijaaj-Gepouja
lineage left the Mapia region to occupy vacant land in the southeastern part of
the Kamu Valley. In summary then, another important difference between the traditional and the localized unilineal kinship groups is that the former are rather
static and subject to very slow change; the localized groups are dynamic, their
relationship and status being in a constant, although often slow, state of flux.

CORPORATE NONUNILINEAL KINSHIP GROUPS   The smallest segments
of which the Kapauku societal structure is composed are the nuclear and polygynous families. Their common criteria of membership are consanguineal and
marital kinship ties and a common residence. In the Kapauku society these
groups perform economic, reproductive, elementary educational, and socializa-

tion functions. Although the judicial and political powers of the husbands and fathers are considerable, in their over-all importance they appear only secondary to those of the political and legal authorities of the more inclusive kinship groups.

It is an ambition of almost every Kapauku to have a polygynous family. However, since women have to be paid for, a polygynous family is an institution that reflects the economic status of the father and is one that not all the natives can afford. The number of wives varies with the wealth of the husband, and may, in extreme situations, reach even ten. Economically speaking a Kapauku polygynous family does not form an undivided whole. From the point of consumption and distribution this unit constitutes a conglomerate of its constituent quasi-autonomous nuclear families. Kapauku individualism prescribes not only separate quarters for the co-wives, which they share only with their children, but also separate finances and plots in their husband's gardens. These they work independently consuming the produce only with their own children. They surrender, of course, a portion of the food to their husbands. Although there is little sexual jealously among the co-wives, this lack is compensated in the economic field. Consequently it is imperative for a husband who desires peace in his home to be impartial in assigning land plots to his wives and in distributing gifts of meat, salt, ornaments, or money. Reflecting the cultural emphasis on equality and personal freedom, all co-wives, irrespective of their age and the sequence of their marriage, are regarded as equals. It is only the husband who may punish a misbehaving wife by a reprimand, beating, or (in serious cases such as adultery), by wounding or killing with an arrow. If she regards his treatment as harsh and unjust a wife may leave her husband by divorcing him. In her disciplinary and educational functions a woman wields power over her own children. However, she has no right to castigate her stepchildren, nor has she the power to control her sons once they are older than seven years. At this time the jurisdiction over the boys is fully transferred to the father.

In the field of production the polygynous family forms a distinct entity. It is the husband who is the central planner and coordinator of these economic activities. It is also he who has to take care of most of the man's work in the gardens. In order that the production of food proceed smoothly, he induces his wives and children to do their share of work adequately and on time.

The Kapauku nuclear family is almost always an integral part of a larger unit, such as a polygynous family, extended family, or household. In exceptional cases it may be independent and form a separate household. Of the 16 households of the village of Botukebo, for example, only one is composed of a single nuclear family. Within the larger groupings the nuclear family performs several functions of its own that set it off from its societal surroundings. In addition to its sexual and procreational roles it functions as an important unit of social instruction and control of the child, in which the young Kapauku receives his elementary education (in etiquette, technology, and food production). Ideally speaking, the father is the head of the nuclear family. He is expected to punish offences of his wife and children (if not older than approximately nine years) with scolding, reprimand, or beating with the hand or a stick. Only in very serious offences, such as his wife's adultery, is he allowed to take extreme measures, such as wounding or killing the culprit with a bow and arrow. Since no one in the whole society, except the head of the nuclear family, has a right to punish a married woman or a child, he is held legally responsible for the crimes committed by his dependents. This is, of course, an ideal picture of the power relations within this smallest of the Kapauku kinship groups. There are families, however, in which the father and husband is only a figurehead, while the actual power rests with his wife. For example, Pigome Oumau, a very strong-willed and clever woman, definitely wields power over her husband and children. However, despite the fact that she is the individual who makes the important decisions in the family, she never forgets the conventions of Kapauku culture. Toward outsiders she always acts as if her decisions were those of the supposed authority—Ijaaj Jikiiwiijaaj, her husband. Once Jikiiwiijaaj was reluctant to sell me some pork. In the middle of our negotiations appeared his wife who, unlike her husband, was of the definite opinion that they should accept the shell money I offered for the meat. With a pleasant smile and a sweet voice she cunningly interrupted our conversation by saying: "Actually he (Jikiiwiijaa) wants to sell the pork, but it takes him always so long to make up his mind, is it not so?" Her husband "encouraged" by another of her smiles, accompanied by what I would call a rather stern look, agreed meekly with his wife's interpretations of "his actual desire."

In the sphere of economics the nuclear family is a unit of consumption only so far as the wife and children are concerned. The man has to supply all his wives and children with food that he produces (certain garden products such as pork, game, and salt), and he must even share it with the rest of the males of his household. Thus the man is also a member of the larger consumption unit of his polygynous family and household.

RESIDENTIAL GROUPS   Unlike the other groups of Kapauku society, membership in residential groups depends exclusively on residence, without any reference to the mutual kinship affiliation of the members. Whereas these groups play a minimal role in the field of social control and law, they all perform important functions in the native economy and education.

One of the two types of Kapauku residential groups is the village. It is a loose conglomeration of houses, usually about 15 in number, built wherever their owners choose, provided they have secured a proper title to the plot (ownership or lease). There is no well-defined plan in a traditional Kapauku settlement. The inhabitants, usually numbering around 120 individuals, for the most part belong to a single patrisublineage, or nonsubdivided patrilineage. Consequently, while there are nonsubdivided lineages whose members live in only one village (such as Dou lineage of the village of Bunauwobado), there are also lineages and even sublineages whose many members live in several villages situated in the lineage or sublineage territory (for example, Ijaaj-Jamaina sublineage members live in Aigii, Jagawaugii, and Kojogeepa villages). In addition to the male members of the local patrilineal kinship group with their in-marrying wives and children, a Kapauku village population also includes some in-law relatives of the males, apprentices, and political dissidents from other groups, all of whom may belong to other patrilineal groupings. All these people refer to themselves as "residents" of a particular village (for example, Botukedo *bagee,* residents of Botukebo). Whereas the village and the surrounding territory represents home for the members of the local patrilineal sublineage and lineage, the other individuals are outsiders who had to secure political permission in order to establish their residence in the community. Such permission is often granted by a tacit consensus of the important men.

A Kapauku village may be regarded as a permanent settlement in the sense that it persists for a long time in a given area. However, the village has a tendency to "move" slowly in one direction or another. As the place becomes too smelly and the houses old and dilapidated, the Kapauku build new structures, often using the old material, on nearby "clean sites." In exceptional cases a village may be transferred in an abrupt and organized fashion from one place to another. No matter how it moves, its new site must always be located on the sublineage or nonsubdivided lineage territory. Since a Kapauku village is fully integrated into the local patrilineal kinship group, which provides it with leadership of a single or several headmen, it is politically and legally of little importance, but it performs several significant economic and social functions. For example, construction of large structures from which all or many of the residents of a community benefit, such as a main drainage ditch, a large fence, or a bridge, is planned and organized by the village as a whole. However, the most spectacular function of a village is its organization and sponsorship of large economic events such as *juwo,* the pig feast, *tapa* the fund-raising ceremony, and *dedomai,* the pig market. All these events are of tremendous economic and social importance. Their success not only brings wealth to the residents of the community, but it also provides them with entertainment and high prestige.

The population of a Kapauku village lives in smaller residential units called *uwougu,* the households. Members of a household sleep in one *owa,* a large house, and one or several *tone,* small houses for women. Whereas all males of the same household (older than seven years of age) sleep in *emaage,* a common dormitory that occupies the front half of the main house, each married woman with children expects to be provided with separate quarters. These may be either *kugu,* partitions in the main house, or *tone,* small houses with single rooms.

The composition of a Kapauku household varies widely in its mutual relationships and the size of its membership. Approximately one third of the households combine the houseowner's extended family with several distant consanguineal or affinal relatives, apprentices, or very distantly related political refugees. However, there exist many other types of residential groups that, in their composition, range from a simple nuclear family, through various forms of extended families, to the most comprehensive type described above, which I propose to call "augmented family" (a family augmented by one or several distantly related kinsmen). As to its size, a Kapauku household may comprise from 5 to 40 residents. The owner of the house is the titular head of the group. He is expected to admonish and punish with private reprimand, beating and, in serious cases, with expulsion those adolescent and adult male members of his residential group who misbehave. Except for his own children, wives, and other female members of his polygynous or nuclear family of orientation, he has no direct control over the rest of the coresiding females and children. The jurisdiction over these individuals belongs to their husbands, fathers, and brothers. With a rich houseowner may reside one or several "apprentices." These are usually distantly related or even unrelated boys and young men who come to live with the prosperous man to receive from him a "secondary education." This consists of learning trade, evaluation of money, profitable ways of investment, and so on. For this service, and for the shelter and food, they help their teacher and landlord in food production and trade. They constitute some of his most reliable supporters in political and legal disputes.

A Kapauku household functions to some degree also as a production unit. The head of a household is expected to assure a steady and balanced diet for all his coresidents. This he accomplishes by coordinating the production and harvesting activities of the individual nuclear and polygynous families who live in his house. But he can only persuade his followers to perform their work; he can never enforce his decisions. The food that is consumed is "shared" by the members of the household in the sense that a man who harvested some vegetables or fruits, or secured meat and game, functions as a host to the rest of the household. His coresidents are expected to reciprocate in kind in the near future.

ECONOMIC GROUPS   In the Kapauku societal structure there is only one type of group whose function is exclusively economic. It is the "gardening unit" whose members work together on agricultural production. Since, exceptionally and temporarily, a gardening unit may also be composed of a single individual, I hesitate to call this unit of Kapauku agricultural production a "gardening group." In 1955, for example, there were 43 gardening units in the village of Botukebo. Of these only five consisted of single males, all of whom were young men, adolescents, or even children. Because all of these individuals will ultimately marry, it is obvious that this type of gardening unit is transitory. Usually a gardening unit is composed of a man who is the owner of several gardens, and his dependents who, having no gardens of their own, help the garden owner with his work. These dependents, who may number anywhere between 1 and 15 individuals (or sometimes even more), are usually close or distant patrilateral, affinal, or (rarely) matrilateral relatives of the garden owner. Thus a gardening unit often constitutes a nuclear, polygynous, extended, or augmented family. A rich man's dependents frequently include apprentices who are either very distantly related to their "teacher," or not related at all. As to age and sex, most of the dependents are either females, or young and very old males. Since men past adolescence and those of middle age are expected to have gardens of their own, one seldom finds such individuals fully dependent for food production on someone else. In the village of Botukebo, for example, there exists only one such case. Two adult single men, having no gardens of their own, help their brother Kamutagajokaibo, to till his land.

The head of a gardening unit is the owner of the gardens cultivated by that group. He determines the sites for new plots; clears them (sometimes with help of others) of trees and brush; fences them; and drains them by a proper system of ditches. He selects the proper crops to be planted, and sees to it that they are well cared for and harvested on time. For the help rendered by his dependents he owes no payment. Instead of a monetary reimbursement the members of his gardening unit have a right to harvest crops for their own consumption. If, however, any of the dependents (especially adolescent sons and apprentices of the garden owner) conclude a special labor contract with the head of their gardening unit, by which they pledge to make a garden by themselves, they have to be paid in the same way as any other hired laborer.

POLITICAL GROUPS   The Kapauku inventory of segments of societal structure includes federations of localized lineages and political factions. Because both of these types of groupings define their membership and functions exclusively along political and legal lines they can be called political groups. Two or more localized Kapauku lineages, that may belong to different sibs, unite themselves for defense as well as offense into political confederacies. Their membership, which may range from 400 to well over a 1000 persons, resides in a number of villages, which in the Kamu Valley almost never exceeds 9. I have chosen to call these political units "confederacies" because the individual, constituent, localized lineages of such a group have a kind of political autonomy that allows them to remain neutral and abstain from war waged by the rest of the confederated lineages. In very exceptional cases a lineage may even switch its alliance to another federation of lineages. However, since I have not been able to find a single example of such a shift, this ideal appears to be purely academic.

A Kapauku confederacy is the most inclusive politically organized group. Within such a unit law and order are administered by a hierarchy of native headmen; beyond this group no political organization exists. Interconfederational relations are characterized by what one may call diplomatic negotiations and, if these fail, by wars. At the head of every confederacy stands one (in rare cases two or more) native headman. Such an individual as a rule is also the leader of the strongest constituent lineage of the confederacy. It is his duty to see to it that all disputes between the constitutent lineages are settled peacefully and that no feud disrupts the unity of his following. To this effect he often assumes the role of a chief justice and adjudicates the disputes. In addition to his role of keeping peace within the confederacy, he represents his political unit in the realm of interconfederational politics. Here he tries to settle disputes with outsiders through deals and negotiations conducted with political leaders of the pertinent confederacies. If these diplomatic contacts fail to bring satisfactory results, the headmen are faced with the problem of war. It is usually their word and opinion that carries most weight at meetings that are held in order to decide whether one should tolerate an interconfederational injustice or resort to fighting. Similarly, it is they who carry the burden of deciding upon cessation of hostilities and who must arrange effective peace negotiations.

The Kapauku informal political leadership depends primarily on the wealth of the individual and his generosity in extending credit to his followers. Since there may be two or more individuals of the same wealth and degree of generosity in any of the politically organized groups, multiple leadership is by no means a rare exception. The Ijaaj-Pigome confederacy presents two such examples. There the Dou lineage of Bunauwobado has two leaders who together carry amicably the burdens of political administration and jurisdiction. They are Onetaka and Akoonewiijaaj, two wealthy brothers, who in friendly cooperation try to shape the political destiny of their lineage. Similarly, the numerous Jamaina sublineage has three strong men who share peacefully their political and judicial powers. However, such peaceful cooperation between colineages of the same group is not always the actual state of affairs. Since human personalities sometimes prove to be incompatible, instead of understanding and cooperation one may find strong rivalry between the competing headmen. If the two leaders reside in the same village such rivalry has an important effect on the structure of the Kapauku society. In this case the community becomes divided into two hostile camps, and the followers of each of the headmen form an organized group that I propose to call a "political faction." Within such a group disputes are easily solved through adjudication by the leader. Relations with members of the other faction are usually not so good, often being marked by violent verbal disputes and even fights with long wooden poles and sticks. Needless to say, such an unfortunate situation weakens the group internally, becomes a drain on the finances of the villagers, prevents organized construction of large village structures (such as main drainage ditches and fences, bridges), and makes the group less resistant to pressure and attack from outside. Approximately 10 years ago the Ijaaj-Enona sublineage, a subgroup of the Ijaaj-Pigome confederacy whose members reside in the village of Botukebo, split into two opposing factions, one led by Dimiidakebo, the other by the old headman, Awiitigaaj. Their rivalry often disrupted the village life and resulted in violent outbursts of stick fighting. With the death of the former, Botukebo was once more united under the seasoned and shrewd leadership of the aging Awiitigaaj. The followers of the deceased Dimiidakebo often recall their leader's wealth and powerful personality; however, even they recognize that, with the elimination of the village factionalism, community life became more prosperous and enjoyable.

3

Political Organization

Power Relations Between Individuals

"KAPAUKU HAVE NO CHIEFS or any other type of leadership. They form the most democratic society that I know of, in which every man is equal to everyone else," said a European who had spent several years in the Kapauku territory to me upon my arrival to New Guinea. It would appear then that here was one of those mysterious societies that are claimed by Western observers to exist without leaders and, consequently, without any political organization. Another European, who basically agreed with the statement quoted, qualified it, however, in an important respect: "There is a man who seems to have some influence upon the others. He is referred to by the name *tonowi*, which means 'the rich one.' Nevertheless I would hesitate to call him a chief or a leader at all; *primus inter pares* would be a more proper designation for him." By his words, "the first among equals," he understood an individual who, although equal to the rest of the members of the society (who did not recognize him as a leader), happened to be first among them in a common activity. No matter how pleasing such an explanation of the concept *tonowi* may appear to those determinists who, following Durkheim, try to separate society from the individual, it does not account for the fact that the same individual repeatedly, in many separate actions, happens to be the *primus*. Neither does it elucidate the reasons why others vie to become followers of such an individual.

The claim of a virtual absence of leadership in the Kapauku society and the denial of a leadership role to the *tonowi* rest not only upon a narrow, Western-biased conception of leadership, but also on a misinterpretation of the native egalitarian philosophy and the social control achieved among these Papuans by inducement rather than by compulsion and force. Western people usually conceive of a leader as an individual with a substantial amount of power who issues his decisions and orders to his followers in a rather formal way. If,

47

however, one does not insist on compulsion and formality, the absence of leadership among the Kapauku appears illusory.

Unlike Western society, Kapauku social control is not based upon compulsion. The people place a high value upon individual independence and freedom of action. As explained in the section on religion, they even believe that such freedom of action and absence of compulsion is essential not only to man's well being but to his very existence. Since deprivation of freedom is regarded as inhuman and is claimed to result in the death of the deprived, this Papuan society does not know the institutions of jail, war captivity, serfdom, or slavery. One does not force anyone by torture or physical harm to conform to a prescribed behavior. A dangerous criminal or a captured enemy is killed but never tortured or deprived of his liberty. A culprit may be punished by beating or shooting an arrow through his thigh, but during the administration of these penalties he always has a chance either to fight back or to run away. If he does not do so, it indicates that he prefers to accept the punishment and then resume a normal life among his people. In a society with these notions and practices one cannot expect to find enforcement of laws and edicts in the sense that one is accoustomed to in the West. Inducement rather than physical compulsion is the main agent of social control here. A child, for example, may be spanked for mischief, but is not forced by beating into behaving properly. Sanctions work as inducements for better behavior in the future rather than as an immediate enforcement. Similarly, a decision of a Kapauku leader is most frequently not issued in the form of an order and enforced physically; it is made in the form of an opinion or suggestion and the followers are persuaded into an acceptance of it. Because wealth is one of the highest goals of an individual, inducement very often takes an economic form. Fines and withdrawing and extending credit, or a threat of these, are some of the most frequent types of political and legal incentives to conformity.

Leadership in the three smallest types of Kapauku groupings, the household and the polygynous and nuclear families, is defined formally. In the household it is the house owner who wields the power of leadership, while the authorities in polygynous and nuclear families are defined on the basis of kin and marriage bonds (father, husband). Unfortunately, such formal criteria of authority and leadership are absent in the rest of the more inclusive Kapauku groups. In all of these there exists only one type of authority, a rich man, whom the natives call *tonowi*. Because he is an informal authority with a limited amount of power, who achieves his status through personal endeavor and success rather than by having it assigned to him, he should be labelled "headman." The Kapauku headman is distinguished from the rest of the members of his group by a set of the following personal criteria: wealth, generosity, eloquence and verbal courage, physical fitness, bravery in war, and shamanism. The first three criteria should be considered basic and indispensable for the achievement of the status of a *tonowi*, the fourth is only conditioned by one of the three preceding, and the last two should be regarded as nonessential (an individual may assume leadership without them) but power-enhancing.

As was documented in the chapter on technology and economy, Kapauku place a high value on wealth, from which they derive their greatest prestige. Consequently it is not surprising that economic considerations constitute the most effective inducement to conformity, and that extension of credit is a primary factor of social control. Thus wealth is prerequisite for attaining and keeping political leadership. People satisfy the wishes and comply with the decisions of a wealthy man. They do so because they are the man's debtors and are afraid of being asked to repay their loans, or because they expect some future financial aid, or they are grateful for past financial favors. For the followers of a wealthy leader compliance with his requests and decisions means economic security. Since wealth depends upon successful pig breeding and trading which, in turn, are affected to a great extent by the state of the individual's health, age, or quality of judgment, the political structure and leadership pattern in the Kapauku society is in a constant flux. New individuals emerge as influential leaders only to lose their position some years later to younger and more successful pig breeders and traders.

Wealth by itself, however, does not make a Papuan a leader of his people. Not all rich individuals acquire followers and can issue weight-carrying decisions. Hoarding wealth does not carry prestige; indeed in some regions, such as that of the Paniai Lake, selfish and greedy individuals, who have amassed huge personal properties, but who have failed to comply with the Kapauku requirement of "generosity" toward their less fortunate tribesmen may be, and actually frequently are, put to death. For example, during my first research in the year 1955, a wealthy man named Mote Juwopija of the village of Madi failed to be generous in proportion to his huge fortune. People of his village, dissatisfied with the state of affairs, spoke to the first paternal parallel cousins of the greedy man and persuaded them to kill him. In order to avoid any future feud the would-be executioners, by promises of monetary advantages as well as threats of excommunication, induced the eldest son of the delinquent to join the firing squad. This finally consisted of five men who ambushed the unfortunate wealthy man in his garden on the third of August and shot him to death. Even in regions such as the Kamu Valley, where such an execution is not a penalty for greediness, a nongenerous wealthy man is ostracized, reprimanded, and thereby finally induced to change his ways. In the whole Kapauku territory generally, a man who acquires his property improperly through theft, borrowing without repayment, or embezzlement, or a selfish individual who hoards money and fails to be generous, never sees the time when his word is taken seriously and his advice and decisions followed, no matter how rich he may become.

Under the term "generosity" the money-minded Kapauku do not, of course, understand gift giving. As we have seen, the institution of "gift proper" does not constitute part of the native economy. The term refers rather to extensive money lending, often without charging interest. Only such an extensive money lender becomes a political leader and is regarded as a highly moral individual. Thus the economic institution of credit plays a basic role in the political as well as legal life.

The emphasis on generosity, and the severe consequences attached to its absence, cause the natives to become very secretive about their personal riches. While they are quite willing to discuss their loans, they are most reluctant to disclose the amount of their savings and cash, so that no one will ask them for a loan or charge them with selfishness. To acquire data on personal savings and available cash was one of the most difficult tasks of my research. I succeeded only because I inquired into the individual's fortune in complete secrecy, assuring him that I would neither disclose the information to other people nor ask him for a loan. As a positive inducement for compliance with my requests I made it perfectly clear that I liked and regarded highly a man with cash on hand, and that only upon such an individual would I most likely bestow a monetary "gift in the Western sense." Although the Kapauku considered me a very strange individual who threw his money around, they nevertheless exploited my "foolishness" and told me about their fortunes or even displayed them to me.

Wealth and generosity are, however, not the only prerequisites for political leadership. Ijaaj Timaajjokainaago of Botukebo, although a very rich and generous man, failed to attain leadership because of his shy personality and fear of speaking at public gatherings. About three quarters of my informants from his village thought he would make a splendid leader "if only he would speak up." Despite wealth and generosity, a man who is afraid to argue publicly and pass judgments, who lacks eloquence and verbal courage, has little chance of becoming a Kapauku headman.

In addition to the three basic personal requirements for leadership—wealth, generosity, and verbal courage—an overwhelming portion of the headmen exhibits a fourth characteristic that is conditioned by the requirement of wealth. Since ill health and old age inhibit mobility, attentiveness to business and, in general, economic efficiency, a native headman is as a rule healthy and middle-aged.

Whereas the first three personal characteristics of a native headman have to be considered basic and indispensable to the attainment of leadership, and the fourth one is conditioned by the characteristic of wealth, bravery in war and shamanistic power are additional, nonessential, but power-enhancing attributes. Not all the Kapauku headmen can boast of being brave and possessing supernatural power. Because in time of war a brave headman need not delegate his leadership to an expert warrior, his influence over his followers is obviously greater than that of a *jape weda tonowi,* a cowardly rich man. Similarly, a headman endowed with shamanistic powers possesses additional important means of social control. Shamanism is highly valued by the natives, and the skilled practitioner occupies a status second only to the headman. If the *tonowi* happens also to be recognized as a shaman, his prestige reaches the highest peak in the Kapauku society.

Personal relations between the headman and his followers may be of various kinds. Since financial considerations form the highest inducement toward conformity, the most dependable of a *tonowi's* adherents are his debtors. Their fear of being asked to pay back money they have borrowed, coupled with gratitude for the headman's generosity, makes them their benefactor's stoutest supporters. They can always be depended upon in war or in a legal suit. With respect to war, the death of a wealthy man does not release the debtor from his obligation; unfortunately for him, debts and credits are inherited. Since one almost always has personal and, as a rule, cordial relations with the man who loaned the money, whereas one cannot depend upon the generosity of the heir, the debtors are vitally concerned in the life and welfare of their rich creditor. This becomes even more understandable when one realizes that most frequently upon the death of a rich man his heir asks the debtors for immediate repayment of their loans.

Besides the debtors a wealthy man has usually several additional ready supporters in his apprentices, whom he calls *ani jokaani,* "my boys." These young individuals usually come from poor families and join the rich man's household in order to obtain from him a good education in business administration and politics, to secure his protection, to share his food and, finally, to be granted a substantial loan for buying a wife. For these favors, in turn, they offer their labor in the gardens and around the house, their support in legal and political disputes, and their lives in case of war. These young men function often as bodyguards; by their physical presence alone they elicit respect for the rich man and induce other individuals to respect his wishes. It would be a mistake, however, to regard these young men as some sort of serfs of the *tonowi.* The contract of apprenticeship is quite loose and allows both parties to terminate it at any time. The apprentices are never treated as inferior by the rich man. They have the right to be fed, protected, and provided with shelter as long as they offer their benefactor their support and their (usually not extensive) labor. Since a *tonowi* is only morally obligated to his apprentice to grant a loan toward the purchase of a wife, either side is free at any time to sever the contractual relationship.

As with every Kapauku individual, the headman also finds important support among his *imee bagee,* "the kinsmen." These individuals are induced to follow their rich relative because of an emotional bond as well as because of a network of duties, rights, and expectations of future reciprocal favors. It is always good for a Kapauku to have a headman as a close relative because one can depend upon his help in economic, political, and legal matters. The other followers of a *tonowi* recognize him as a leader and accept his decisions as binding either out of gratitude for his past generosity or because they expect future favors and economic advantages.

A Kapauku *tonowi* functions as a political leader in conducting diplomatic negotiations with representatives of outside units. A *tonowi* in the role of a leader of a whole political confederacy decides matters concerning war and peace; within the group he functions as an authority in disputes among his followers. It is especially in this field of social control that the leader's role as a judge, negotiator, enforcement agent, and trouble extinguisher becomes most important for the smooth functioning of his group. However, the multiple functions of a *tonowi* are not limited to the political and legal fields only. His word also carries weight in economic and social matters. He is especially influential in determining proper dates for pig feasts and pig markets, in inducing specific individuals to become cosponsors of feasts, in sponsoring communal dance expeditions to other villages, and in initiating large projects, such as extensive drainage ditches and main fences or bridges, the completion of which requires a joint effort of the whole community.

Power Structure of the Society

Kapauku society is composed of many types of subgroups of different inclusiveness. Each of the subgroups has its own leader who differs from leaders of other subgroups in his personality, experience, amount of wealth and power, and rank. The personal criteria of a headman define a Kapauku individual as *tonowi,* the political and legal authority. However, these criteria do not designate his rank in the hierarchy of headmen. A simple comparison of the amount of wealth of two headmen certainly fails to indicate which is superior to the other by his command of a larger group. In order to determine the rank of a particular *tonowi* one must turn to the societal structure and its criteria for the different types of authorities.

Every Kapauku headman has two statuses which correspond to the two aspects of social organization as presented in the previous chapter. Whereas his social status as a headman is determined by the personal criteria just discussed, his social status in the hierarchy of the various types of headmen is defined by his membership in particular subgroups of the society and by the web of their mutual relations. The social status, furthermore, determines the headman's amount of power, his scope of jurisdiction, and the type of law he is supposed to administer. Principles regulating the social status of a *tonowi* may be summarized as follows. First, every functioning subgroup of the Kapauku society has a leader whose rank depends on the inclusiveness of that subgroup. The headman of a confederacy is, consequently, superior to the headmen of the constituting lineages, and these, in turn, are superior to the leaders of the component sublineages. Second, holding the position of headman of a more inclusive group depends on simultaneous possession of a headmanship in one of its constituent subgroups. Thus political statuses are cumulative. Accordingly, for example, a headman of a whole political confederacy, the most inclusive political group, occupies also a position of *tonowi* of one of the constituent lineages and sublineages, and is the head of his household. The number of his followers, the amount of his power, the intensity of his control, and the kind of law he has to administer differ in every instance. Third, a principle of the societal structure determines which of the headmen of groups of the same category becomes the authority of the higher, more inclusive group. Accordingly, that *tonowi* who comes from the most populous of those subgroups which together form a group on the immediately higher level of inclusiveness, assumes the headmanship of this higher, over-all group. This may be documented in the case of the Ijaaj-Pigome confederacy, a political unit of the southwestern part of the Kamu Valley. There Ijaaj Ekajewaijokaipouga, the leader of that confederacy, comes from its strongest constituent subgroup—the Ijaaj Gepouja lineage. Within this group he is the headman of its strongest and most numerous Ijaaj Jamaina sublineage. Because of the third principle, Ijaaj Awiitigaaj, the powerful and ambitious leader of the Ijaaj Enona sublineage (which is another component of the Ijaaj Gepouja lineage) cannot become the confederacy's leader, despite the fact that his village is the largest one in the whole confederacy. His sublineage, which belongs to a level that is immediately lower than that of the lineage, is weaker than that of Ekajewaijokaipouga. Within his sublineage the confederacy headman resides in the largest village of Aigii. There he possesses the largest household of all his village coresidents.

Since headmanship in a group requires the achievement of wealth, the display of generosity, and the eloquence of a candidate, it sometimes happens that two, or in very rare instances even more individuals, who come from subgroups of the same importance, qualify in the same degree for the position. In such an instance all assume equally the power and jurisdiction in the group. In most cases their condominium is marked by a full cooperation and respect for each other's decisions. Jurisdiction over a given case belongs to that particular headman who comes to the scene of a dispute first and begins his adjudication. The other "cooperative" headmen leave the decision entirely to the first *tonowi*, supporting his pleas and decisions when needed. Since not all personalities are compatible, however, there do exist coleaders who do not tolerate each other and even exhibit marked mutual disrespect and hostility. Such rivalry within a group may split it into competing and antagonistic political factions, which weakens the solidarity and, consequently, the power of the group as a whole. However, this factionalism and discord is usually confined to internal problems of the unit. In disputes with outsiders the split groups unite, and the wealthiest of the coheadmen acts as representative of the group.

The largest and most inclusive of the Kapauku groups that is politically organized is the confederacy. It always consists of two or more lineages that belong to the same or different sibs, whose members, numbering anywhere from a few hundred to several thousand, have allied themselves for defense and offense into a political union. The territories of such allied lineages usually lie next to each other, thus making the confederacy a territorial unit. This union is always more or less loose, limited to the political sphere, and has no economic, educational, religious, or other social functions. Within this unit, law and order are administered by the confederacy headman and the leaders of the constituent subgroups, who do not concern themselves with war and the diplomatic relations of the union. The confederacy constitutes a unit in warfare, which almost never occurs between its component subgroups.

Legal Structure

The law of a primitive society has traditionally been portrayed as a single, well-integrated legal system with preferably no judicial deviations from the prevailing rule; but such a smooth, relatively static, and simple picture of primitive law is definitely unrealistic in any of the functioning societies because it fails to take into account one of the most important factors about law: namely that it always, of necessity, reflects a particular societal structure—the segmentation pattern of the society in which it exists. There is no social group or subgroup that does not possess leadership and regulatory devices for the conduct of its members. Thus the societal structure not only determines the rank of a specific authority but also creates a configuration of legal systems of the society's subgroups. According to the types and inclusiveness of the various groups, the corresponding legal systems form a hierarchy. Within such a hierarchy we find on the same level legal systems of groups of the same inclusiveness. Thus in the Kapauku society we have legal levels of confederacies, lineages, sublineages, households, and families. Law not only varies within a given legal level, for example from one family to another, but different, sometimes even contradictory regulations exist in legal systems of different legal levels. Since a Kapauku individual is simultaneously a member of several subgroups of different inclusiveness (such as the family, household, sublineage, lineage, and confederacy) he is subject to all the various legal systems of these groupings. Consequently he may be ruled, and often actually is, by several legal systems differing to the point of contradiction. An outstanding example of differences in the content of legal systems of related groups occurs in the Ijaaj-Pigome confederacy where it affects the regulation of incest by its subgroups (Pospisil 1958b : 19–20). In one of the confederacy's lineages incestuous relations between members of the same sib were punished by execution of the culprits, and in another by severe beating, in the third constituent lineage such a relationship was not punishable and, as a matter of fact, was not regarded as incest at all. In one of the sublineages it became even a preferred type of marriage!

The difference between the various legal systems and between the various legal levels are not limited to the content of specific laws. They occur also in the use of particular types of sanctions and in the types of adjudicated offenses. So, for example, the use of some particular sanctions is restricted to specific legal levels. Accordingly, the head of a Kapauku household cannot sentence an individual to death; slapping and beating with the hands as a punishment for delicts are confined to the family and household levels. Payment of blood money and confiscation of all property are sanctions used by the authority of groups that are more inclusive than the household. The settlement of adjudicated offences is also in many instances confined to specific legal levels. Thus breaches of etiquette, verbal insults, and quarreling are delicts punished only by the head of a family. Similarly, disputes resulting from refusals of economic cooperation are adjudicated only on the lowest legal levels of the family and household. But war crimes such as treason, desertion, or other types of disloyalty during hostilities are brought exclusively to the attention of the headman of the entire confederacy.

When such marked differences exist among legal systems of the same political confederacy, one can easily imagine what profound discrepancies in law may exist between legal systems of two such different groups. Nevertheless, despite the differences in the various systems of law one may point out some generalizations that pertain to the field of Kapauku law as a whole. Although the Papuans possess a very informal and simple political organization they do have abstract notions of proper behavior pertaining to a variety of situations. These notions are verbalized into abstract rules which they call *daa*, meaning actually "prohibitions." These verbalized precepts are conveyed to the memory of wise men in such a standardized form that several informants may independently cite some of the rules "verbatim," their versions being the same almost to the word. In my book on the law of the Kapauku (Pospisil 1958*a* : 144–247) 121 such rules are listed. However, the wise men and the *tonowi* did not remember only the abstract rules for conduct; they also used their profound knowledge of a body of legal decisions that had settled disputes of the past. That this additional memory was important for a Kapauku "lawyer" is documented by the fact that of 176 disputes (Pospisil 1958*a* : 144–247), settlement of only 87 corresponded to the pertinent rules. In other words about 51 percent of solutions passed by the native authorities disagreed with *daa*, the abstract rules of the Kapauku "mental legal codification."

Another striking aspect of the Kapauku law is its secular character. Of the 121 rules only 14 of them have anything to do with the supernatural. All of the 14 rules concern delicts resulting from magic or breaking a supernaturally sanctioned taboo. As far as the actual disputes are concerned, only 7 of the 176 I recorded dealt with offences against the supernatural. Kapauku law indeed seems to be preoccupied with economic matters. Of the 121 rules, 70 regulate economic relations, and of my 176 cases, 91 were concerned with purely economic delicts. Furthermore, Kapauku conceptualize economically many other delicts which Western jurists would classify as family and personal law, or crimes against persons. Thus, for example, rape and adultery are regarded by the Kapauku as delicts of a basically economic nature: a man used a woman without properly "paying for the license to have an intercourse" with her. Accordingly—both rape and adultery are termed *oma magii,* "theft of sexual intercourse."

In addition to these special attributes Kapauku law protects and emphasizes the native notions of individualism, while exhibiting an alarming lack of concern for the "group's or society's interests." Offenses against persons, such as murder, battery, and manslaughter, are regarded primarily as private delicts, settled between the parties concerned, thus not deserving the application of our term "crime." Of all the recorded rules and cases of disputes only six rules and seven disputes dealt with group (public) interests.

External Political Relations

In Western civilization the term *law* has been traditionally applied to rules for behavior, promulgated either by a whole nation or a state. Such a set of rules is regarded in the West as the primary standard to which an individual tries to conform, and upon which he depends for his protection. In the Kapauku society, however, there exists no authority that would unite inhabitants of two or more valleys. Indeed, this society not only lacks an over-all political organization and authority, but law and order do not transcend the boundaries of political confederacies. Beyond these political unions only diplomatic negotiations and war prevail. The lack of tribal or national law is here forcefully demonstrated by the fact that all wars that I have recorded have been fought among the Kapauku themselves.

In order to understand the power mechanism underlying diplomatic negotiations between the confederacies, which are carried on by the authorities of these units, reference must be made to the Kapauku social structure. The societal structure cannot be of any help in this respect, because those groups that do carry political importance are either identical or smaller than the political confederacy. On the other hand, those groups that transcend the boundaries of confederacies, and thus cut across them (such as consanguineal kin groups), lack political functions and consequently are not pertinent to this consideration. The Ego-centered quasi-groups of the social structure, on the contrary, whose members form temporary unions while acting on behalf of a specific individual (Ego), carry significant intra- and interconfederational political functions. As we have already seen, the relatives, debtors, apprentices, and friends of a headman, who happen to be members of his confederacy, are his most dependable followers, being linked to him through social and economic bonds. Their relatives, friends, and debtors, in turn, support the authority's decisions because of their indirect dependence upon him. Consequently, a clever Kapauku politician selects as his debtors and best friends those individuals who themselves possess many followers. Thus, indirectly, a wealthy man, through relatively few direct bonds of credit, marriage, and friendship can command the following of a multitude. In selecting as his debtors and friends the most influential individuals from the various subgroups of his political domain, a headman of a Kapauku political confederacy strengthens his power and influence and reinforces the political structure of his unit. In the interconfederational politics a shrewd Kapauku *tonowi* behaves in a similar manner. He selects especially influential headmen of other confederacies as his debtors and friends. If his attempts at making these men his debtors or friends fail he has another means at his disposal: through the institution of polygyny he can easily make them his in-law relatives and thus his supporters in interconfederational matters. Ijaaj Ekajewaijokaipouga of Aigii, the headman of the Ijaaj-Pigome confederacy, has built up in this way such an important and extensive network of relationships based on economic, friendship, and marriage bases that it spans virtually the whole Kamu Valley. Thus his word and decisions are often respected in quite remote parts of this region. Strangely enough, he also acquired as best friends, debtors, and in-law relatives important men from among the traditional enemies of his own political unit. Consequently, even in times of hostilities and war his influence in the hostile confederacies persists, and provides convenient channels for negotiating a peace. In addition to the function as go-betweens who help to negotiate peace, the headman's friends, debtors, and in-law relatives, as well as those consanguineal relatives who reside beyond the boundaries of the headman's confederacy (for example maternal consanguineal relatives), help the headman in peaceful settlements of interconfederational disputes, which otherwise would develop into wars. In this function of settling of interconfederational disputes the quasi-groups resemble international courts of justice, and the principles of arbitration that through long usage are applied to relations beyond the scope of law proper, appear comparable to our modern "international law."

As in the civilized world so among the Kapauku, the "international law," unlike the true intraconfederational law, does not often succeed in peacefully solving problems and settling disputes. Thus these diplomatic negotiations form no quarantee for eliminating conflicts between individuals from different political confederacies. When negotiations fail, the aggrieved party usually has two choices: he can either tolerate the injustice and accept the humiliation of being regarded by his neighbors as a coward, or he can decide on taking an "honorable" way out of the deadlock and declare war on the enemy. Because the Kapauku are proud and self-respecting people I was able to record in detail 11 recent wars, and collect more sketchy data on an additional 26 armed conflicts.

No Kapauku seem to like war. Unlike many of the lowland Papuans, the Kapauku culture places emphasis on the economic success of an individual and regards war as a necessary evil that destroys rather than increases economic assets. "War is bad and nobody likes it," claimed Ijaaj Jokagaibo, one of the headmen of the Ijaaj Jamaina sublineage. "Sweet potatoes disappear, pigs disappear, gardens deteriorate, and many relatives and friends get killed. But one cannot help it. A man starts a fight, and no matter how much one despises him, one has to go and help because he is one's relative and one feels sorry for him." A war may last only a few days and result in few casualties or it may become a prolonged affair, disrupting the normal life of the Papuans for a period of several months, and may even account for the death of several hundred warriors. During my stay in New Guinea in 1955 I witnessed two wars; one lasted only one day, while the other continued for about one month, interfering seriously with my supply line from Lake Paniai to the Kamu Valley. Several informants reported that about 15 years prior to my first research there was a war in Egebutu, in the southwestern part of the Kamu Valley. The hostilities lasted for over a year and the numbers of the dead exceeded 250, leaving one of the involved communities, Degeipige, practically without any adult male inhabitants. The number of participants in a battle also varies. In one engagement only about 80 warriors may be involved; in another combat a 1000, or even more men may participate.

The cause of a war among the Kapauku can always be traced to a dispute between individuals from two different confederacies. In the Kamu Valley the cause of such disputes and, consequently, the cause of the resulting wars is most frequently a divorce, initiated by a woman who has deserted her husband. Although killing by the use of sorcery accounts for most of the hostilities in the neighboring Mapia region, it ranks only second in the Kamu Valley. Of 11 wars of the Kamu on which detailed informations are available, 5 were caused by a divorce initiated by the wife or her brother, 2 occurred because of witchcraft, 1 was caused by an accidental death, 2 had economic causes (stealing and embezzlement), and 1 started as a children's game of arrow shooting which, through an accident, developed into a serious conflict.

A war is usually begun by a party injured in an interconfederational dispute. He either tries to secure military support for his cause by pleading with the headman of his political unit, or he may neglect this slow but correct procedure and precipitate a war by starting the fight himself and inducing his relatives and friends to aid him. During the ensuing hostilities he is called *jape ipuwe* "owner of the enemy," and is held, to some degree, responsible for the consequences of the conflict. If he started the war without the approval of the headman of his confederacy, and if his reason for fighting is regarded as unethical, he may risk capital punishment passed upon him in a secret conference by the *tonowi*. The verdict is usually executed by the close paternal parallel relatives (brothers and patriparallel cousins), who ambush the man and kill him with arrows. However, if the cause is considered just and the *jape ipuwe* secures the support of the appropriate political authorities, a regular war starts by an attack against the enemy's villages. Despite the attempt of the aggressors to keep the offensive a secret, an individual from the hostile camp invariably discovers the approaching war party and warns his people of the danger by yodeling *jape meete, jape meete,* "the enemy is coming, the enemy is coming." Upon this warning men rush from the houses and nearby gardens to meet at an open place in the village. Invariably the approaching enemy yodels to them the reason for the attack and the conditions under which they would be inclined to suspend the hostilities. At this moment there is still time to avoid bloodshed and come to terms. Unfortunately, in many cases both sides claim they are right and the war begins. The defenders perform *waita tai,* a counterclockwise circular dance in which, shouting at the top of their voices, they run in a circle, carrying their bows and arrows in their hands. Then, led by the war leaders, they hurry to meet the enemy, preferably in an open grassland, where they try to stop him short of the village. There, two parallel battle lines are drawn up which move back and forth as the fighting progresses.

The Kapauku fight exclusively with bows and arrows. They use no hand weapons, such as spears, clubs, or daggers. As a consequence, the fighting resembles modern warfare in several aspects. The natives do not mass themselves to an attack or defence. On the contrary, they fight almost individually, most of the time taking cover in the tall grass and bush. From their hideouts they emerge to discharge their arrows. The braver warriors, however, do not hide. They prefer to avoid the oncoming arrows by *kokogai,* "jumping from side to side," thus not providing the enemy with a static target. Some of the "less brave" combatants carry shields made of planks in their netbags; these, suspended from the tops of their heads, rest on their shoulders and backs; to protect themselves from the flying projectiles they have only to turn their backs to the enemy.

Since the meager supplies of ammunition are quickly exhausted, it becomes the duty of the women to collect stray arrows for their husbands. For this task they have a generally agreed-upon immunity that protects them from the enemy. The Kapauku consider it highly immoral for a man to shoot at a female during a battle. Even an accidental injury brings to the unfortunate warrior derision and loss of prestige. He is constantly reminded of his mistake and taunted even by his own people and relatives: "You better stay home and don't fight; all you can do is shoot a woman." The women exploit this situation to the limit. When I saw for the first time a Kapauku battle I could hardly believe my eyes. While the men were engaged in deadly combat, and dead and wounded warriors were being carried away, many of the women, obviously undisturbed, were quietly collecting arrows on, behind, and between the battle lines, as if they were harvesting potatoes or cucumbers. Several of the bolder members of the "weaker" sex even climbed a hill behind the enemy's lines and, from there, shouted advice concerning the enemy's movements to their fighting husbands. The annoyed and embarrassed enemy could only try to chase the women away by pushing them or beating them with bows and fists. Aside from the mortification of having to contend with the women, the warriors were often not even assured of success in routing them because the women wielded walking sticks, usually much longer than a bow, and it was sometimes the men who received the pushing and beating.

While the married women are protected by rigorous custom, unmarried girls are fair game for those warriors who come to help the enemy with the fighting (such as enemy's friends, and in-law and maternal relatives). When I expressed shock over such ungentlemanly behavior my friend Ijaaj Jokagaibo of Itoda explained: "There is nothing to be sorry for. These girls like it anyway and some may even get caught willingly. During an attack on Degeipige, I raped a beautiful girl. She screamed and wept all right but this was only a pretense. After the cessation of hostilities she came after me to Aigii and asked me to marry her." Indeed, in such situations when unmarried girls, under various pretenses, appear close to the attacking enemy, it is always questionable whether one should label the resulting sexual acts as rape by the males or seduction by the girls.

The regular fighting takes place during the day. It begins early in the morning, when the people perform their familiar *waita tai* dances, and then depart in a group for the battleground. While they are marching to meet the enemy, the women, because of their immunity, walk on the flanks, ahead and in the rear of the warriors, thus protecting their men from the arrows of snipers. By walking far ahead of the fighting force the women also function as scouts. Upon arrival at the area where fighting takes place the warriors form the battle lines, arrows start whizzing through the air, and the women busy themselves collecting the stray ammunition. In-law relatives of the fighting men may either join the warriors on the battlefield, or they may manufacture arrows, supplying their relatives with needed ammunition. Old men and children are left at home where they either occupy themselves with producing arrows or with agricultural tasks or swine-herding.

This regular type of warfare is occasionally interrupted if one side starts winning by having succeeded in killing a few enemies; the other side is then forced to a hurried retreat toward its village. The retreat may be temporarily halted behind a protective cover near the houses if the defenders have erected a barricade made of short planks driven vertically into the ground. If the defense proves ineffective the victorious invaders plunder the gardens of their enemies, burn their houses, and kill all the pigs they can find. After the devastation is complete, the invaders withdraw with their loot, which consists of killed pigs, garden crops and, possibly, some shell money which they might have found in the abandoned houses. For those warriors who succeeded in killing enemies the day becomes especially memorable. After having shot a lethal missile, a successful killer performs *ukwaa wakii tai,* a killer's dance. He runs around in a small circle, holding his bow at its lower end in the right hand, and twists it by the movements of his wrist. He accompanies this dance by joyful screams, *"wuii-wuii,"* emitted at the highest pitch of his voice. This performance, which is put on despite the danger from flying arrows, is for the purpose of drawing attention to his success so that there will be no question of his identity when he claims his reward for killing the enemy. To celebrate his feat the successful warrior gives a feast called *me nai,* "to eat a man," in the evening on the day of the killing. Although the name may suggest cannibalism, the feast bears no trace of such practices. The celebrated killer simply slaughters his own pig, cooks its meat, and distributes it to his relatives and friends.

In addition to the fighting on the battle lines a Kapauku warrior can prove his skills in another way. As a sniper he may penetrate deep into the enemy's territory and shoot an enemy from ambush. His victim may be a male of any age: a warrior in the prime of life, a very young boy, or an old man. On his expedition the sniper may be accompanied by several of his relatives or friends who provide him with protection on his way into the enemy's territory, and who also cover him during his retreat after his mission has been accomplished. However, the last few hundreds of yards to the enemy's village, and during the actual assault, the sniper is alone. His supporters wait for him at a distance from the enemy's settlement. This is done not so much to prove the skill and courage of the sniper, as for a practical consideration: whereas a party of several warriors can easily be detected, a skilled single sniper might well succeed in escaping the attention of the enemy.

When both sides are tired of warfare, and when there is an equal number of dead on both sides, it is time to start peace negotiations. The quasi-groups of in-law relatives of the confederacy headmen are usually employed for this purpose. These men function as go-betweens who arrange the conditions for an armistice. After this is accomplished, peace is formally concluded at a pig feast when the former enemies dance together in front of the dance house. The gathered multitude is then addressed from the roof of the structure by its leaders, who declare cessation of hostilities and urge their followers to live again in peace.

War among the Kapauku is not exclusively a political problem. Economic aspects of the conflict have to be taken into consideration in order to fully understand the cause and conduct, as well as the conclusion of hostilities. To the Kapauku mind divorce, elopement of a married woman, and death of an individual are as much economic problems as theft, embezzlement, or breach of contract. If a married woman, for example escapes with a lover and he reimburses her husband in the amount of the bride price that was originally paid for her, there is usually little hostility and animosity. Similarly, if the killer of a man properly pays the blood money prescribed by custom, the grieving relatives are easily placated. It is always in cases in which these proper payments are refused that war ensues.

In addition to these economic causes an armed conflict has also quite formalized economic consequences. With war are connected special types of payments that are well defined by custom, and are enforced by the authorities. Except for one type of payment, the well-known blood money that is paid to the enemy as a compensation for the death of one of their relatives, all other types of transfer of goods take place within the same political group. From the multiplicity of the various types of payments one can easily realize the economic emphasis that the Kapauku place upon war.

It has been pointed out that one of the most important prerequisites for concluding peace is that the number of dead people on both sides be the same. This condition is referred to as *uta-uta,* a balance (lit.: "half-half"). Any discrepancy in the numbers will either preclude a peace agreement or will require a monetary compensation called *me mege* (lit.: "human cowries"), which may be translated as blood money. This is a rather onerous indemnity consisting of at least 180 old Kapauku cowries, 180 introduced cowries, and 2 fully grown pigs, paid as a compensation for the death of a single man. These goods are transferred by the *jape ipuwe* (lit.: "the owner of the enemy") of that side having the advantage in the number of dead, to the father and brother of that individual from the enemy's camp whose death remained "not avenged." While the brothers may keep the pigs, the rest of the payment is distributed among the more distant relatives of the dead warrior. The problem of payment of blood money is complicated by the fact that any individual who dies after the peace is concluded, of a wound received in the war, upsets the *uta-uta* balance, thus requiring a new payment in order to re-establish the equilibrium. Many an individual who has suffered an injury in war makes a public statement that an arrow fragment has been left in his body. The native surgeon who tried to extract the projectile usually testifies to such a pronouncement. No matter when such a person dies, his heirs are then entitled to lay claim for a blood money payment. Since some such claims are made even twenty or more years after the end of a war, it is not surprising that the justification of such claims is questioned and, as a consequence, the payments often refused. Such refusals, needless to say, frequently constitute a cause for "resumption of hostilities." During my last research in the year 1962 Keija Ipouga of Bunauwobado died, supposedly because of a fragment of arrow which a surgeon had failed to extract from his body approximately twenty years earlier. The relatives of the deceased man, led by Ijaaj Maatabii of Aigii, a father's mother's brother's son of Keija, made a claim for payment of *me mege* against Tagi Tagikabii of Tuguteke, the son of the late Tagi Kumeebedo, the man credited with the ancient injury to Keija. Tagi refused to pay the required sum on the ground that there was no proof that Keija died of the injury inflicted on him by Tagi's father. Indeed he challenged the relatives to an autopsy to prove that a splinter was actually left in the old wound of the deceased. At the time of my departure negotiations were still in process. It appears, however, that the UN or the new Indonesian Administration will either have to adjudicate a very difficult dispute or face a war in the Kamu Valley.

This case was complicated by another kind of payment, called *uwata*. This type of monetary transfer may be designated "blood compensation." It consists of a payment made by the *jape ipuwe*, "the owner of the enemy," to the closest relative of a slain man who fought on the side of the *jape ipuwe*. This obligation, which amounts usually to 120 old Kapauku cowries and 2 pigs, must be fulfilled within three days after the slaying, or the *jape ipuwe* may risk a severe punishment. He may be either turned over to the enemy, or some of his pigs may be shot and confiscated. In compliance with these customs the descendants of the *jape ipuwe* on whose side Keija fought, the Dou people of Bunauwobado, delivered to the relatives of Keija the traditional *uwata*. The sum actually paid deviated from the traditional amount because a monetary equivalent was substituted for the pigs required by custom. Thus relatives of Keija received actually 145 old Kapauku cowrie shells, and 105 introduced cowries. This voluntary payment made by the progeny of the Dou *jape ipuwe* is being held as an argument by the Keija's relatives against Tagi Tagikabii, the son of Keija's "killer." It is claimed that since the progeny of the *jape ipuwe* admitted and paid their obligation of *uwata* it is obvious that the request for *me mege*, the blood money, which is to be paid by Tagi, is justified.

A third type of payment connected with war is called *dabe uwo* (lit.: "mud water"). Since it is a reward paid by a relative of a slain man to a warrior who avenged the man's death by killing an enemy, I feel justified in translating the term as "blood reward." This payment takes place upon the request of the successful avenger, and is made after the war is ended, sometimes even several years later. Because the reward often amounts to considerable fortune, the collection of it takes place in a formal fund-raising ceremony called *tapa*. On the day of the ceremony a multitude of relatives, friends, debtors of the *tapa ipuwe* (lit.: "owner of the *tapa*"), and the man who sponsored the ceremony and who is obligated to pay the blood reward, gather at a specified village and contribute, ceremonially, their shares to the collected wealth. The next day the reward is transferred to the lucky avenger. An idea of the size of such a payment can be obtained from the reward paid by the Pigome people of Obajbegaa to Ijaaj Jokagaibo of Aigii for killing Jobee Ibo of Bauwo to avenge the death of an Obajbegaa man: 60 iron machetes and axes, 60 long strings of glass beads, 3 *dedege* (necklaces of small cowrielike shell), 2400 large glass beads, 240 old Kapauku cowries, 600 introduced cowries. This wealth is enough to purchase 31 medium-weight pigs. Because Jokagaibo is a most generous headman, who seeks popularity, he turned over the whole amount of collected goods and money to his friends and relatives, not keeping a single shell. Such generosity in disposal of a blood reward is not, however, always the rule. Accordingly, Ijaaj Awiitigaaj, the shrewd headman of Botukebo, made this statement with regard to the problem of generosity: "They can have their praise and respect, I do not care for them. I prefer to collect and lend the money. This way one becomes rich and the debtors are dependent anyway. I am a headman not because the people like me but because they owe me money and are afraid."

Death of an individual often requires two additional expenditures to be made by the main heir. First, the heir is held responsible for the payment of *emoo mana* (lit.: "blood words"), which has to be made to that individual who held the wounded man in his arms at the time he died. The payment is rationalized as being justified not because of the comfort given to the dying man, but as a compensation for the danger to which the individual who holds the dying man in his arms is exposed. The Kapauku believe that such a man may be infected by the blood of the dying warrior, become stomach sick, and eventually die. For running such a risk he is therefore entitled to receive *emoo mana* in the amount of ten Kapauku cowries. Another payment, called *peu-uwo* (lit.: "bad water"), is due to the individual who buries a dead man. The heir of the deceased is usually liable for the sum of approximately two old Kapauku cowries for the service of the native "undertaker."

4

Ceremonial and Spiritual Life

Ceremonies

WHEN COMPARED with the elaborate rituals of the lowland Papuans, the Kapauku ceremonies appear indeed unimpressive and simple. One does not find here any art, such as wood carving, painting, or complex, well-patterned dances that are connected with the performances. Unlike that of their lowland neighbors, Kapauku ceremonial life is characterized by simplicity, lack of emphasis upon conformity with a rigid pattern, and a marked stress on secularity and sobriety. Whereas the ceremonial events among many primitives are concerned mainly with the spheres of religion and the supernatural, among the Kapauku almost all the most important ceremonies are connected with their economy. The main purpose of these is not a manipulation of the supernatural in order to effect some material advantages for the performers, but rather an achievement of the desired economic effects directly, by placing the ceremonial emphasis upon the secular economic transactions themselves. Consequently, an overwhelming number of ceremonies have to be classified as purely economic in their nature. Even such ceremonies of the life cycle as birth, marriage, and death have strong economic motivations and overtones. The wedding ritual itself consists actually of a ceremonial gathering and transfer of the bride price from the husband's party to the relatives of the bride. The bride has little to do with the "wedding"; in most cases she is actually absent. Of all the ceremonies the magical ones, which include the only ritual connected with the supernatural, are the least elaborate and spectacular; their purpose in most cases is either to cure or to kill by witchcraft.

Kapauku ceremonies fall into three categories: life cycle, tribal economy, and religion, but these categories do not imply rigid mutual exclusiveness. As has been said, most of the rituals of the first and last categories have indeed important economic functions, and many of the economic ceremonies also play important roles in the native life cycle and incorporate magical elements.

LIFE CYCLE CEREMONIES   The Kapauku birth ceremony is a rather simple affair. It consists of a feast given by the father in honor of his newly born child. Everyone who comes is treated to pork or the meat of rats or large marsupials. As a minimal requirement for this occasion the father is expected to prepare at least eight large pieces of pork, each weighing approximately six pounds, or ten large marsupials. He and his father, the paternal grandfather of the child, prepare the meat in one or several *dopo*, "cooking mounds," steaming it together with fern leaves and other vegetables by means of preheated stones, in a bundle made of long reeds and pandanus leaves. The food is usually prepared in the *emaage,* the men's common dormitory of the father's house. When cooked, the meat is cut into small pieces and distributed to the male guests who either squat around the mound or, because of lack of space inside of the house, are gathered outside around the entrance. To the females, who stay in the women's quarters in the rear of the building, the food is handed through special openings in the wall between the rooms. The people eat, talk, joke, and also discuss more serious political and economic issues. They may stay long into the night, some of them even spending the entire night with their proud host. A few days later the mother of the baby, in turn, gives a birth ceremony in honor of the child at her parents' home. The procedure is the same except that it is not so conspicuous, and the mother of the child is the host. In the women's quarters she prepares the food, which has been provided by her father and brothers, and passes it to the males gathered in the men's dormitory in the front of the house.

The birth ceremony has actually two main functions: it celebrates the birth of the child, and thus introduces it formally into the society, and it is an occasion for the host to increase his economic and political prestige through generous and lavish distribution of food. The greater the number of guests and the greater the amount of food distributed, the greater the prestige of the happy father. Since his political importance will persist and his lavish spending on his guests will be reciprocated, the birth ceremony may be regarded as a profitable economic enterprise.

Except for the first hair-cutting ceremony the child is not subjected to any ceremonial treatment until he reaches puberty. The first hair-cutting ceremony is performed by the father who cuts the hair and shaves the child's head with a bamboo knife. After this task is completed, and the hair hidden in the bush to protect the child against possible sorcery, the proud father gives a feast to his relatives and friends by treating them to steamed pork. The ceremony has no magical connotation; it celebrates the child's growth and health and provides the father with an opportunity to prove his generosity.

Although there is no puberty ceremony for the boys, first menstruation becomes an important event in a girl's life. At such an occasion her father, brother, parallel cousin, or (if she is married) her husband builds her *daba owa,* "a menstruation hut." This simple structure consists of an oblong frame of sticks, leaned against two posts, and thatched over with grass and branches. The girl is expected to stay in the hut for two nights and two days during her first two menstruations. In the hut she is kept company by two or three older women who may be her mother, older sisters, brothers' wives, mother's sisters, or father's sisters. During this time the girl is instructed by her custodians in marital duties, birth, child care, and in the observance of taboos connected with menstruation and womanhood. These taboos are of two categories: one is connected exclusively with the puberty ceremony, the other consists of food taboos which the girl, now considered an adult woman, will have to observe until the beginning of her menopause. Accordingly, during her first two menstruations she is forbidden to sleep, listen to legends, and leave the hut. Should she violate these taboos her punishment will be supernatural: if she sleeps she will suffer from nightmares; if she listens to legends she will have to bear the early death of her husband; if she leaves the hut, she will suffer a great illness. Sickness will also result, it is believed, from her eating any kind of wild game, banana, sugar cane, native beans, manioc, and certain kinds of caterpillars. The strictest supernatural sanction–that of inevitable death–is attached to the taboo, which prohibits the menstruating girl from washing herself or combing her hair. Throughout her child-bearing years she will have to refrain from eating *teto,* the red sugar cane, *apuu,* a type of yam, and two types of plantains called *jigikago* and *kugou.* These prohibitions are sanctioned supernaturally. Upon her violation of them her husband would inevitably die, and she would be held legally responsible for his death and would be punished by her husband's relatives with execution. At the close of the ceremonial seclusion the girl is expected to hide the leaves into which she collected her menstrual blood in order to prevent a sorcerer from harming her by the use of contagious magic. At this time she also exchanges her loose girl skirt for an adult woman's loin wrap.

In most societies the ceremony that marks the start of married life and is called a wedding, usually centers around the groom and the bride and their unification. One would seek such a wedding among the Kapauku in vain. The only ceremony distinguishing the marital life of the couple from their previous livelihood has nothing to do with their unification. Indeed, in most cases the bride, who is already living with her new husband, is absent. In some cases even the groom does not participate in the ritual. It actually consists of a ceremonial collection of the bride price, and of its transfer from the groom's to the bride's party. In its essence, then, it should be classified as an economic ceremony. The name wedding seems to be justified only because the transfer of the wealth does seal formally the marriage of the young couple, which invariably has been consummated some time before this occasion.

Although many Kapauku marriages start with elopement, a proper marriage procedure is expected to begin with a conference between the groom, who is usually supported by some of his relatives, and the bride's kinsmen. The discussion between the suitor and the parents of the girl concentrates almost entirely upon the amount of the bride price. The welfare of the bride and her desire to marry her suitor are either taken for granted by both sides or, if an aversion of the girl to the man is well known and manifested by her explicit refusal, means are discussed by which to overcome her resistance and make the prospective union more acceptable to her. Such difficulties are frequently accompanied by economic repercussions: the prospective groom is asked to pay a bride price that is higher than would normally be the case. Sometimes the girl's mother may actually safeguard her daughter from marrying an undesirable man by asking a forbiddingly high price. Fortunately, such difficulties are exceptional. Most discussions about the amount of bride price follow a proper courtship, and sometimes even a short period during which the couple have already lived together and cohabited.

After the price and the date of its payment have been agreed upon, and thus the preliminaries to a marriage concluded, the groom concentrates upon collection of the bride price. This consists of two parts: *one*, the main payment, composed of the old and most precious Kapauku cowries and pigs; and *kade*, an accessory to the first payment. *Kade* consists of inexpensive, introduced cowries, *dedege* "shell necklaces," introduced glass beads, and a few manufactured articles, such as large shell necklaces, net bags, and axes. While the *one* part of the bride price is composed of the groom's own cowries and a few large contributions made by his patrilineal relatives, the *kade* payment represents numerous small gifts contributed by the groom's relatives and friends. The contributions to *one* are regarded as loans that have to be repaid in the future. The donations to *kade* are considered gifts which ought to be reciprocated, not upon the request of the donor, but in the form of *kade* when the donors or their close relatives are married.

From the ceremonial point of view there is also an important difference in the way the two payments are collected. The *one* part of the bride price is gathered informally from the paternal relatives of Ego, each single loan being transferred into the possession of the prospective groom individually and at a different time; all the *kade* gifts are payable ceremonially on a single specified day called *kade makii naago* (lit.: "the day when *kade* is laid down"). On this same day the already gathered *one* is publicly displayed on pandanus rain mats, and is later formally surrendered to the bride's relatives. An average bride price consists of approximately 120 old Kapauku cowries, 120 introduced cowries, 300 glass trade beads, 3 *dedege*, "shell necklaces," and 1 large male pig.

The preparations for the *kade makii naago* starts when the groom with his father and brothers visit their patrilineal relatives to collect loans toward the *one*. On these occasions the groom's party announces the date of the "wedding" and invites to the occasion as many people as possible. When the ceremony draws near the groom and his close paternal relatives make special expeditions to various villages to remind everyone of the wedding date. The ceremony itself begins on the stated day at approximately ten o'clock in the morning when the father, brother, or mother of the groom places one or two rain mats in front of their house. Often the *one*, which has already been collected, is laid on the mat for public inspection. Early in the morning people begin to arrive from all directions in order to act either as contributors or simply as spectators to the ceremony. The bride's relatives usually arrive all in one group. Their procession is augmented by many of their more distant relatives and friends who are prepared to support the bride's kin in case a dispute over the amount of the bride wealth develops. At the gathering they usually keep together, squatting in one group near the mats with the bride wealth. Frequently the amount of shell displayed fails to meet their expectations, and one can immediately guess their displeasure from their somber expressions. Off and on one or several of them rise, move slowly to the mats to inspect the shell and, after having exchanged stern looks and a few derogatory remarks concerning the quality of the shell and the quantity of the gathered total, they return to their places.

At this time the contributors come forward to deposit their shell, beads, or necklaces on the mats. Female and male friends and relatives rise from the various squatting groups and silently approach the displayed bride price in order to add to it their own treasures. Since the expression on the faces of the members of the bride's party remain stern, the local headmen begin to worry about trouble which may arise any time. In order to forego a dispute or even possible violence they make long appeals to the relatives of the groom, soliciting greater contributions by playing upon their relations to the "poor groom" and appealing to their pride, as generous and well-regarded individuals. They remind them that if the expectations of the bride's party are not fully satisfied, the young man faces a possible loss of his bride. In order to make their appeal more dramatic, the headmen may start *wainai*, "a mad dance," by stamping the ground with their feet and holding their left arms outstretched and the right arms bent at the elbow, as if they were ready to discharge imaginary arrows. While stamping furiously in a fast rhythm, they yell and scream their requests to the gathered audience. In their endeavor to increase the contributions the headmen are not alone. At some point the father, brothers, or paternal uncles of the bride join in the tumult with reproaches and insults hurled, not so much at the already insolvent groom and his close paternal relatives, as at their more distant kin and friends, trying to make them feel ashamed of their lack of generosity. If these performances fail to elicit the desired effect, the men of the bride's party are forced into the mad dance themselves, thus posing a real threat of breaking up the negotiations. If this should happen the bride would be taken away from the groom and the latter charged with a payment of *pituwo*, a fine of 3 to 5 old Kapauku cowries paid for using the girl sexually out of wedlock. In extreme situations even an outright fight may develop from an unsatisfactorily conducted wedding procedure.

The atmosphere is filled with emotions, threats, danger, and especially with a grave challenge to the reputation of the friends and kin of the groom. No matter what they think about the adequacy of the already assembled bride wealth, they may find themselves reaching into the corners of their netted purses and pulling out additional precious shell and necklaces. As if in a trance they move to the mat, squat, and surrender their treasures to the displayed bride price, perhaps to regret their generous deeds later, when they have cooled off. As more and more individuals experience this ecstatic generosity, the loud appeals and voices of the headmen and the bride's relatives soften, and their angry looks are finally replaced by very faint smiles of satisfaction. Their pleasure over the collected bride price is not, however, made explicit. The Kapauku are never supposed to show too openly their enjoyment over a business deal because one can never tell whether the other party might not make an even more attractive offer. The groom, now assured of the success of his wedding, dries his tear-stained eyes and presents his new in-laws with the promised one or two pigs. The whole ceremony is concluded by approximately three in the afternoon. Individuals who contribute after this time, it is believed, would violate a supernatural taboo and, as a consequence, be afflicted with a disease.

Waka edai, buying a wife among the Kapauku, is certainly not equated with buying a chattel such as a pig. The payment of the bride price has several important social as well as economic aspects. The mother's part of the bride price (which consists of glass beads and shell necklaces) provides her with an important means for elevating her status. By lending part of her newly acquired wealth to her husband or sons she makes them dependent upon her. From now on they had better respect her wishes or she may ask for the return of the loans. The payment received by the bride's brother provides him with the means to buy himself a wife. The father of the bride, who in the Kamu Valley is not supposed to keep anything from the price paid for his daughter, referees the adequacy of the bride price and its distribution. Thus he reconfirms his importance as the head of his family, and earns admiration from his sons as well as from the public for his skill in making the groom's party pay a high amount. The contributors to the bride price gain not only public prestige for their generosity, and gratitude from the groom for their help, but they also have had a good opportunity to make a safe loan which is well publicized and is secured by a mortgage placed upon bride prices to be paid in the future for the daughters of the bride whom they have "helped to buy." The gratitude of the groom to his creditors is so great that it finds formalized expression in the address that the groom is expected to use from now on: he has to call all these creditors *naitai,* "my father." He also is expected to give unqualified assistance to them in their future political and legal disputes. To a rich groom the payment of the bride price offers an opportunity of increasing his prestige by paying more than the amount originally agreed upon. He thus not only enhances his political status but also strengthens the marital bond, because the higher the bride price, the less chance there is that the wife's relatives will side with her in marital arguments or support her in obtaining a divorce. Should she leave her husband they would have to return the entire bride price. Such a repayment would certainly represent an economic loss, because they could hardly expect to collect as large a sum from another suitor. In this respect, then, the appropriate or high bride price has a stabilizing effect upon the marriage.

The life cycle of a Kapauku individual is concluded by a funeral ceremony; as soon as the soul leaves the body, relatives of the deceased give a formal expression to their grief. They weep, eat ashes, cut off their fingers, tear their garments and net carrying bags, and smear their faces and bodies with mud, ashes, or yellow clay. The most conspicuous manifestation of grief is a loud sing-song lamentation that is called *jii jii tai*. In order to give more publicity to his sorrow a bereaved mourner climbs a hill or a cliff where he laments and weeps as loudly as his vocal cords will allow. His *jii jii tai* is carried by the winds through the valley, announcing the sad news to all the relatives and friends in remote villages. Obedient to the message, the relatives smear their faces or even their bodies with clay, mud, or ashes. They hurry to the place of death and rush into the house of the deceased; wailing loudly, they beat the hearth in the men's dormitory with a long stick. They believe that in so doing they punish the spirit of hearth, who dwells underneath the stone fireplace, and is believed to consume the body in the grave. Its ghoulish orgy is manifest to the Kapauku by the decay of the corpse. Sooner or later one of the *maagodo noogei*, best friends of the son of the deceased," arrives and presents his mourning friend with a large pig. This is killed in the afternoon and its meat distributed to the mourners and their friends during a funeral feast in the evening.

In the afternoon the in-law relatives of the dead usually bind the corpse by its arms and legs to a pole and carry it in a procession to the place of burial. The disposal of the body is, as a rule, an affair in which only a very few close relatives and friends of the bereaved family participate. Often the place of the burial and the time of the procession to the grave are kept secret. At the beginning of my research I attributed this secrecy to Kapauku religion and magic. Later, however, the real reason for this observance became apparent. Since every man who comes and mourns the dead at the grave on the day of the burial must be paid by the main heir for his manifestation of sorrow, the heir, in order not to go bankrupt, limits the secret of the burial place, and participation in the funeral procession to a few close relatives and best friends. The necessity for secrecy becomes obvious because there are among the Kapauku professional mourners who participate in as many funerals as possible, collecting handsome payments for their mercenary howling from the unfortunate heirs.

The disposal of the dead among the Kapauku takes many forms because it is felt that an individual should have a burial appropriate to his importance and to the cause of his death. Very young children and individuals who were not particularly liked or important during their lives are completely interred. Children, women, and old people who were considered unimportant during their lives, but were loved by their close kin, are tied with vines into a squatting position and are semi-interred, with the head above ground. The head is protected against the elements by a dome-shaped structure of branches and soil, and against pigs and dogs by a circular fence. A window is left open in the dome in front of the face of the deceased to induce its soul to become a guardian spirit to the surviving relatives.

An adult man, who was loved and respected during his life, and whose soul is desired as a guardian spirit by the surviving relatives, receives a respectable tree burial. Tied in a squatting position, the corpse is placed in a tree house, consisting of a simple platform and a dome-shaped roof of branches, which is provided with a small window in front of the dead man's face. The branches of the tree that bears the hut are all cut off, so that the remaining trunk and a few larger limbs give the appearance of a skeleton. The people believe that as new branches and foilage sprout and cover the tree-burial from the sight of the relatives, their sorrow should subside and vanish. A similar, but very flimsy structure is provided for a child that dies in birth.

Corpses of important individuals of whom their relatives are afraid, and of women who died in childbirth, require a special type of burial. Because their departed souls and shadows are regarded as unusually dangerous, the bodies are placed in the familiar squatting position on a special raised scaffold constructed in the house in which the death occurred. The house is then sealed and abandoned. In this way, for example, was buried in 1960 Goo Oumau, mother of Ijaaj Ogiibiijokaimopaj of the village of Botukebo. During her life she was believed to be possessed by *meenoo,* "a ghoul spirit," and was credited with killing and devouring the corpses of several individuals.

A warrior killed in combat or shot by a sniper is laid flat on a simple platform erected on four forked posts at least five feet high. In order to induce the soul of the dead man to punish the killer through contagious magic, the lethal arrow is left in the wound. In contrast to this burial dead enemies, whose bodies could not be regained by their relatives, are simply piled on a heap of dry wood and cremated. This was the type of burial received by the members of an ill-fated Japanese platoon that tried to enter Kapauku territory during the Second World War.

The simplest burial of all is given to a drowned man. The corpse is laid flat on the bank of the river, a protective fence erected around it, and the body abandoned to the elements.

The most elaborate burial is awarded to a rich *tonowi,* the native head-man. A special hut, made of planks and roofed over with bark, is constructed on high stilts, so that the corpse is protected against animals as well as rain and flood. The body is tied in a squatting position and a pointed pole is driven through the rectum, abdomen, chest cavity, and neck, so that its pointed end supports the base of the skull. So supported, the body is placed in the dead house so that the face appears in the front window of the structure. The cadaver is pierced several times with arrows in order to allow the body fluids to drain away. A corpse prepared in this way invariably desiccates and becomes a mummy. After years have passed and the structure collapses, the skull of the venerated man may be cleaned and awarded a second honor by being placed on a pole which is driven into the ground near the house of the surviving relatives. For this extra care the close patrilineal kin of the deceased believe the departed soul of the dead man rewards them with special protection.

ECONOMIC CEREMONIES   By far the most spectacular and elaborate Kapauku ceremony is *juwo,* "the pig feast." This is a rather protracted affair comprising several major events and innumerable night dancing parties. The whole cycle of a pig feast usually lasts several months. It starts with the decision of a rich man, preferably a headman, to sponsor a feast. He is motivated by the prospect of profits, and by political considerations. By giving a feast he not only sells quantites of meat and earns the much desired shell money, entertains himself in singing and dancing, and gains prestige from his generous loans of pork but, by a successful event, he also undermines the popularity of his rivals within and without the confederacy. Furthermore a spectacular pig feast enhances the reputation of the community, and ultimately that of the whole political federation, and shames the rival political groups. In outdoing the enemy a sponsor of a successful pig feast is considered to have accomplished a "patriotic and moral" deed and often is regarded by his fellow confederates as some sort of a national hero.

Because of the complexity of the undertaking and the numerous tasks to be accomplished the main sponsor, called *juwo ipuwe* (lit.: "the owner of the pig feast") seeks other rich individuals who are willing to act as cosponsors of the affair. If the main sponsor is known for his riches, generosity, and influence he has no trouble in finding people willing to help him. His reputation alone assures the success of the undertaking, of monetary profits, and of a gain in personal prestige. The cosponsors are usually paternal relatives of a younger generation, or younger relatives of the sponsor's own generation (for example So, BrSo, FaBrSoSo, FaSiSoSo, FaBrSoSoSo, yBr, yFaSiSo). The first role of the cosponsors is to secure the help of the young and poor members of the community in making planks, cutting poles and thatch, collecting rattan, and transporting these building materials to the site on which the dance and feast houses will be erected.

After the building material has been gathered together, the main sponsor initiates the building of the dance house by a magical rite which is supposed to assure the success of the feast and bring lots of money to its sponsors. Early in the morning on the *taka wei naago,* the day when the people start building the dance house (lit.: "the day when the forked sticks of the foundation of the dance house are stuck into the ground") the main sponsor goes to the forest where he cuts a tall *onage,* "a willowlike tree." Over the stump of this freshly cut tree he prays to the Creator to grant success to the feast and bring lots of cowrie shell to the sponsors. After this prayer (which has a definitely magical significance) is concluded, the performer sacrifices the intestines of a rat by placing them on the stump. Then the sponsor with his aides, shouting and yelling for joy, run with the cut *onage* tree to the building site. There they plant it, together with a *ti* plant, into the ground next to the place where the main front post that is to carry the ridgepole will be erected. Next to the planted *onage* tree a hole is dug into which rat intestines are deposited, the action being properly accompanied by a magical spell. The hole is then closed by driving into it a single end of a forked stick that will be the first support for the frame of the spring floor of the dance house.

After this proper initiation the people begin to build the dance house. This has a rectangular floor plan, its dimensions being approximatly 7 by 6 meters. It consists of an elevated spring or jumping floor of long flexible sticks, plank walls, and a gabled roof, thatched with pandanus leaves, whose highest point is about 6 meters above the ground. In front of this structure is a vestibule formed by an extension of the gabled roof and the sidewalls. Doors, about 2.5 meters wide, left in the front walls of the vestibule and the dance hall, provide the entrances. The vestibule serves as a rain protection for the dance audience, and fires are also built there in order to provide light and warmth during the cool nights. To provide additional illumination and heat, two rows of small openings (approximately 40 centimeters wide) are left in the spring floor along the two side walls for small fires to be kindled underneath the elevated floor. In addition to the single dance house, every sponsor and cosponsor of the feast builds his own *juwo owa,* "house." This is a simple oblong structure with vertical plank walls and a gabled roof, thatched with long pandanus leaves. The structure serves as a dormitory for the guests from distant villages, as a storage space for the owner's pigs, as a slaughter house and, finally, as the place where meat is sold, cooked, and consumed.

When the construction of these houses is completed, a significant period of about three months begins, during which groups of men and women from any village or confederacy may come to spend a night in dancing and singing. This practice is called *ema uwii,* "going to the dance house." This dancing period is formally opened by *putu duwai naago,* the day during which meat is distributed by the sponsors to their friends and relatives free of charge, and during which the date of the main and final feast is announced. The day is actually a feast in its own right. The sponsors slaughter about eight pigs and distribute small pieces of pork to the multitude. The pigs are killed in the feast houses early in the morning. Groups of people, each representing a village, lineage, sublineage, or even a confederacy, arrive from all directions, running, yodeling, and jumping over the deep mud holes and ditches filled with rain water. Upon their arrival each group performs the familiar *waita tai,* the counterclockwise circular dance, which they follow with *tuupe.* This is a treading dance accompanied by a repetitious song, during which the whole group of people, who are pressed against each other, tread clockwise. Then the people rush into the dance house to jump on the spring floor and to sing an *ugaa* song. This performance starts with barking cheers, while the people, standing on one place, bend their knees in a fast rhythm and make the spring floor go up and down. After a few minutes the singing subsides and an individual begins a solo song that, after a sentence or two, becomes a duet in which a "helper" answers the singer in counterpoint fashion. This duet, lasting only two to three minutes, is followed by a chorus in which the whole group participates. The *ugaa* song is completed by making a barking sound and rocking the spring floor, this introduces another solo singer with his composition. Although the solo, with the duet part, is a poem composed by the solo singer, the chorus part of the *ugaa* is traditional, and may belong to several well-defined types. In his solo performance the initiator of an *ugaa* song suggests which of the familiar types he desires the group to sing. Each of these songs has an important meaning that often has social implications. In an *ugaa* song a man may, for example, mourn his dead relatives, ask an individual for a monetary loan or best friendship, propose a date or marriage to a girl, or challenge a rival to a legal dispute.

After a few of these songs have been presented, a group moves out from the dance house to make room for others who have arrived and are dancing outside. At about nine o'clock in the morning pieces of raw meat are distributed to the male visitors. Afterward, cooking mounds are made in which the entrails of the slaughtered pigs are steamed. Thus prepared, the entrails are cut into small pieces by the sponsors or their close relatives, and distributed to the women and children. In the afternoon the feast is concluded by a conference held by the sponsors of the feast who, aided by experienced and influential advisors, decide upon the time of the final and main feast, which is called *juwo degii naago*. The date may be set anywhere between 60 and 480 days from this conference. Most frequently, however, a period of three months is considered adequate.

This formal opening begins a period during which groups from any village may come in the evening and spend the whole night dancing and singing in the *ema*, the dance house. These nightly entertainments are among the most enjoyable pastimes of young and old Kapauku alike. The young men, in order to impress the girls, prepare themselves properly for the occasion. They paint their faces with red ochre and soot mixed with grease, comb their hair, put on armlets and fancy necklaces, and adorn their bodies with flowers and colorful shrubbery which they insert under their armlets and into their net carrying bags. For defense as well as decorative purposes they carry fancy bows and arrows. They embellish their hair with bonnets of cassowary feathers or with hairpins which hold the gorgeous bird-of-paradise plumes. The girls put on new loin wraps and wear as many shell and glass-bead necklaces as they can carry. On some girls these ornaments are so numerous as to resemble colorful breastplates. The men, followed by the women, gather in the late afternoon at an open place in their village. There they perform the *waita tai* dance, followed by *juu tai*, "yodeling in a barking fashion," and depart swiftly for the village with the dance house.

The group arrives at sunset, yodeling and cheering. Not losing a moment they release their accumulated energy by *waita tai* and *tuupe* dances, performed in front of the dance house. Afterward they rush inside to sing their *ugaa* songs and jump on the spring floor. The floor-jumping keeps up all night. When it becomes dark the fires are lit beneath the floor to provide some warmth and a scanty illumination. Women appear with their burning torches; among them are girls from the village whose male inhabitants undertook the dance expedition, and from the local village who are eager to join the dancing group. Now the dance house and the gathered singing and swinging multitude present a fascinating picture. The place is crowded beyond imagination—literally several hundred people may be packed into the relatively small structure. Most of the spring floor is occupied by the group of dancing men who are pressed against each other in the center. Above this group of deeply bronzed bodies, which in the torch light glisten with grease and sweat, rises a forest of bows and arrows that the dancers hold upright in their hands. The women, carrying lighted torches, march counterclockwise around the leaping men. The rest of the space is filled with male and female spectators. The place is dimly illuminated by the flickering torches and by the small fires that burn beneath the jumping-floor. The vestibule is crowded with spectators and tired dancers, who warm themselves around small fires or roast a few sweet potatoes. Those who desire a more substantial meal or want to take a brief nap retire to the neighboring feast houses where large fires provide more warmth and comfort.

In this fashion the people spend the whole night. One *ugaa* song, accompanied by the jumping dance, follows the other. They carry important meanings and have social consequences. The natives learn from them the news and problems of the village. They also discover important relationships between individuals that otherwise would remain undetected. One can realize then that such a dance is important and interesting, as well as entertaining to the people. In our Western cultural terms, it is as though one were dancing, singing, listening to new poetry, witnessing disputes and matchmaking, reading the newspaper, and participating in a cocktail party—all at the same time. Indeed, the significance of a pig feast and its *ugaa* songs can hardly be overestimated.

Of the various types of *ugaa* songs with their various social implications, the most important for the young men and women are those in which a singer proposes a date or marriage to a girl. The composition is usually a nice poem by which the singer alludes to the beauty of his girl and asks her for a date at a given place or for marriage, by requesting her to leave with him for his home village. The girl to whom the song is addressed is present in the audience or in the group of women who carry the torches. If she rejects the proposal she angrily throws away the torch and without delay leaves the dance house; if she continues to carry the torch or remains standing in the audience it signifies her acceptance of the offer. Later during the night the two young people steal away and either have a date, which means having sexual intercourse in the bush or, if marriage was the object of the accepted proposal, they run to the boy's village. The close paternal relatives of the couple, then, try to make the necessary arrangements for an early payment of the bride price.

This formal arrangement for dates and marriages serves, however, only a few of the young men. Most of them come to the dance to acquaint themselves with girls and to flirt with them informally. The setting is ideal for such an undertaking. The light is dim, the place is crowded, and the girls with their torches have to push through the dancers on one side and the onlookers on the other. As they proceed in a single or double file, the boys have plenty of opportunity to exchange looks and words or jokes with the girls. If a girl seems to be receptive to such approaches, a boy becomes encouraged. Next time she passes he stands in her way so that she has to push him aside in order to keep pace with the other females. This provides the young man with an excuse to retaliate with a push on her next turn around the dance floor. He feels fully successful if the girl screams, or pushes him away, or slaps him. But a rebuke, or silence, or an unpleasant look from the young lady must be interpreted as displeasure, and the boy is well advised to try his suit elsewhere. The bright-colored hairpins of the boys provide another means for flirtation. The girls, who like to have such pins as souvenirs and decoration, snatch them, as they pass, from the coiffures of the boys. The boys, in turn, try to regain their ornaments when the girls reappear in the moving circle. If the torches go out and sudden darkness envelops the crowd, a few bold young men take the opportunity to grab the passing maidens by their breasts. For such an approach the men are struck with fists, slapped, or sometimes even thrown to the floor by the infuriated women. Despite the blows and the resulting bruises these boys feel fine and are regarded by their friends as the heroes of the evening. Their successful exploitation of the darkness will constitute an important contribution to local gossip for the next few weeks.

This is not to assume that it is always the boys who make the first advances to the opposite sex. The pushing and snatching of ornaments is often initiated by the girls themselves. A girl can even be bold enough to propose a date and the inevitable sexual intercourse. The girl does this by secretly slipping a cooked sweet potato into the boy's hand. He understands well what this small token of love means and he watches the girl carefully. When she leaves the dance house he inconspicuously follows her into the darkness, to spend the whole, or part of the night in collecting the highest reward a nightdance can offer to a young Kapauku.

As the day of the main and final feast draws close, the dances in the *ema* become more and more frequent. Some nights are reserved for the women, when they dance and sing the *ugaa* songs, and the men provide light with the torches. The dancing intensity culminates during the night preceding *juwo degii naago*, "the main feast." During the first half of the night the men dance and sing, and the women provide the torchlight; in the second half of the night the roles are reversed. After sunrise, as soon as the heavy dew on the grass and foliage dries out, the sponsors of the feast appear with their pigs. The animals are slaughtered with bows and arrows, or are sometimes clubbed to death, and the butchering begins. The cut pieces of meat and entrails are stored in small partitions in the back of the *juwo owa*, "the feast house," where the people usually go in order to buy it from the pig owners. All during the morning groups of people come from various villages. Upon their arrival they perform the *waita tai* and *tuupe* dances, and follow these with one or two *ugaa* songs in the dance house. When this is done they disperse in order to conduct business. Most of them come either to buy or to sell something. Pigs, tied to poles, are brought by many people who are not sponsors of the feast, but who use the occasion as an excellent opportunity to market their produce. They select a particular spot in the tall grass where they butcher their animals and start selling the meat. Small or large clusters of prospective buyers gather around the places where pork is being sold. Many of the people are not actually buyers, but come to claim repayment for pork that they have "loaned" in the past. Or they may be "borrowers of pork," who promise to repay in kind in the future.

The trading is by no means limited to meat. The people sell and buy for shell money all kinds of products. The most frequent articles traded are pieces of salt, bundles of inner bark for making strings, bow strings of rattan vines, artistically netted and decorated carrying bags, bamboo containers, bird feathers, and ornaments of various kinds. The buyers and traders argue about the quality of the shell money and merchandise, bargain about the prices, and dispute the offers made by their competitors who try to undersell them. Almost everyone enjoys the feast. Those who have concluded satisfactory transactions function as audience to interesting trade disputes, or enjoy themselves by gossiping with their friends and relatives, some of whom they may not have seen for a long time. The politically-minded individuals, especially the headmen, discuss problems concerning interfederational disputes and possible warfare. The Kapauku pig feast is a place where new alliances are agreed upon, possible war plans are worked out, difficult disputes endangering peaceful coexistence are discussed, deliberated, and often settled, and where peace between enemies is formally concluded. In addition, many a war had its origin at such an "economic gathering."

In the late afternoon the trading is concluded and small groups of people, heavy with purchased meat and artifacts or rich in shell money, slowly return to their homes. Many individuals, especially relatives of the local villagers, decide to spend the night in the community. There they will be treated to steamed pork and entertained by discussions which most probably will last late into the night.

A Kapauku pig feast is an impressive affair. On such an occasion there may be as many as 2000 visitors, and the slaughtered pigs may be counted in the hundreds. The trade turnover, in terms of shell money, may be quite considerable. Generally it can be said that the greater the number of visitors and slaughtered pigs, the greater the prestige the sponsors of the feast will acquire. Successful feasts are talked over and remembered by the people for years. Because of its social and political consequences a Kapauku pig feast, although a trading ceremony in nature, surpasses in its significance the scope of economy and becomes one of the central events around which Kapauku public affairs are patterned.

Other social events have developed among the Kapauku in which the economic aspect is primary, and the ceremonial aspect is always secondary in importance, sometimes being almost rudimentary. These events are of two different types. One is called *tapa,* "the fund-raising ceremony," the other is *dedomai,* "a pig market." Whereas *dedomai* appears to be a purely economic affair with only traces of ceremonial observances, *tapa* does preserve ceremonial overtones and thus appears as an intermediate between *juwo,* "the pig feast," and *dedomai,* "the pig market."

In my first monograph on the Kapauku I translated the term *tapa* as "a ceremony of the transfer of *dabe uwo,*" (the reward paid for avenging the death of a relative). During my subsequent research in 1959 and 1962 it became clear that the translation was incorrect. In 1954–1955 the Kapauku still lived in pure aboriginal condition in which wars were part of their normal life. Consequently, there were so many people killed and avenged in the frequent conflicts, that at all the *tapa* ceremonies I witnessed during my first research period the gathering and the transfer of the *dabe uwo,* the blood reward, figured as the essential feature of the ceremony. However, with the enforced pacification, and the resulting scarcity of opportunities for avenging the death of warriors, the sole purpose of the several *tapa* ceremonies I witnessed in 1959 and 1962 was the gathering of money for purposes other than payment of the blood reward. Therefore the true essence of the *tapa* ceremony is to gather funds for any purpose and is not limited to payment of the blood reward.

Like the pig feast, a *tapa* ceremony has a sponsor who is interested in it as an economic venture; he finds some cosponsors, who need money for their own purposes (such as buying a pig for breeding, buying a wife, or payment of *mune* to the foster father for his care and education). At an informal gathering a date for the *tapa* ceremony is set, usually within 180 to 360 days from the day of the agreement. Unlike the pig feast, no special structures are erected; however, from the time of the announcement of the *tapa* until the day it takes place people from various villages do come in groups for night dances, which take place in the open on a lawn in the village of the *tapa* sponsor. These dances are like those described for the pig feast with one very important difference: since there is no dance house, no *ugaa* songs are sung. The dancers, after an initial *waita tai* dance, spend the night in enjoying *tuupe,* the treading dance, which is accompanied by monotonous, repetitive, but pleasing songs. Since these songs, unlike those of the *ugaa* type, have no meaning and no social consequences, the dances are far less significant than those of the pig feast and, consequently, are enjoyed mostly by the younger generation.

The *tapa* ceremony itself takes place in the village of the sponsor and lasts only one day. It resembles a pig feast in that people come in groups, perform the *waita tai* and *tuupe* dances, bring their pigs for slaughter and for sale, and trade their manufactured items for shell money. Unlike the pig feast, the focus of this event is the collecting activity of the sponsors of the *tapa.* They make long speeches in which they exhort their relatives and friends to contribute to the funds they are soliciting. Sometimes they even perform *odija ugaa,* a dance consisting of tiny jumps with bent knees and with legs held together. This performance is accompanied by a song in which the potential contributors are asked to be generous. It is especially the cross-cousins, the in-law and maternal relatives, and the friends of the sponsors who grant the most extensive loans; in order to exhibit their generosity they bring their contributions, especially those to the *dabe uwo,* in a procession in which the shell and beads, strung on long inner-bark strings, are carried suspended from long forked sticks. Upon arrival each group of contributors approaches the sponsors at a treading pace. Very often a woman, who treads backward while facing the carriers of the money, heads the group. The procession ends by a *waita tai* dance, after which the contribution is ceremonially surrendered to the sponsors. In order to make the fund-raising ceremony more attractive the sponsor, and sometimes also the cosponsors, may kill one or several pigs and distribute some of the meat as gifts. The gifts of meat are offered especially to those individuals who come to the ceremony to repay a loan or to grant a new one to one of the sponsors. The fund-collecting ceremony is concluded late in the afternoon when most of the contributors and traders return home in small groups; a few others remain in the village overnight to enjoy freshly steamed pork and friendly conversation.

The least amount of ceremony is attached to a mass exchange of goods called by the Kapauku *dedomai*. Since the main item sold at such an affair is fresh pork, and because the word itself means "to carve up," I feel justified in translating the native term as "pig market." This market is devoid of the elaborate structures, involved formalities, and ritual observances that one meets at *juwo*, "the pig feast," or *tapa*, "the fund-gathering ceremony." A wealthy man who has several pigs to be killed and does not want to wait for a pig feast or *tapa* sponsored by other people, or has no desire to be bothered as a sponsor with the formalities and social trimmings of the two ceremonies, decides to be a *dedomai ipuwe*, the "owner" or sponsor of a pig market. He simply announces the date to the public and invites everybody to come on that day to his village to sell their products and to buy those of other people. On this day no one bothers with any singing or dancing. Everyone acts exclusively as a businessman. As at a pig feast or *tapa* ceremony, many pigs are slaughtered and their meat sold, and a variety of manufactured objects and raw materials are traded by the gathered multitude. Although the occasion resembles a pig feast and does have a few ceremonial aspects, its significance and functions are entirely economic, being limited to a redistribution of goods and shell money through sale and loan contracts.

MAGICAL CEREMONIES   Like anthropologists, the Kapauku distinguish the two broad categories of magical rites: *kamu*, the white magic, and *kego*, the black magic or sorcery. From the functional point of view the broad category of the *kamu* can be divided into curative, preventive, countersorcery, rain-stopping, rain-making, profit-inducing, love-creating, and war magic subcategories. The whole variety of these rites may be performed by any Kapauku man or woman. However, there are individuals who have acquired a reputation for being successful in the white magical art. The people call these experts *kamu epi me* (lit.: "a man who knows white magic"). They acquire their knowledge informally by listening to and participating in magical ceremonies conducted by other shamans. Sometimes a young man may receive a systematic education in this art from a relative or a friend. Nevertheless, the technical skill is only secondary to what may be called "personal call" to become a shaman. It is believed that a shaman must possess several supernatural helpers in order to manipulate the various evil spirits and counteract the spells of sorcerers. He receives them in his dreams or through visions in which he sees the particular spirits who, through their behavior or explicitly, let him know that they are his guardians. A Kapauku shaman usually has several souls and *tene*, the departed shadows of his dead ancestors, as helpers. In addition to these he must acquire at least one evil spirit as a personal guardian. Of the various evil spirits, those who are favored for this task are Tege, the chief demon and the horrible spirit of the woods; Ukwania, his wife; Madou, the powerful water spirit; and Makiutija, the vicious ghost of the earth. These spirits are believed to be able to rout other evil spirits. Obviously, if a man is stricken by a sickness that is diagnosed as the work of a particular spirit, he can be easily helped by the particular shaman who controls the spirit by having him as his guardian. In such a case, a command or bribe by the shaman is all that is needed to stop the evildoing of the ghost. The guardian spirits are essential for the shaman, who has no supernatural power of his own. They tell him about the proper cure in his dreams or visions, or they possess the shaman and talk through his mouth in a high-pitched voice, spitting out the words like machine-gun bullets.

The last, and probably the most important prerequisite of shamanism is social recognition. A man who knows the spells, is about middle-aged, healthy, and known to have cured in the past, is accredited as a shaman. Thus Kapauku are quite empirical about the whole business. A shaman has to prove that he can cure others. Obviously he himself has to be healthy and prosperous or it would be obvious that he lacked shamanistic powers. Ijaaj Ekajewaijokaipouga of Aigii, the headman of the Ijaaj-Pigome Confederacy, can be cited as an example of a powerful shaman. The man is healthy, middle-aged, most prosperous and rich, a superb speaker and performer, and is credited with many cures. He is believed to have 5 departed souls and shadows as well as 12 different evil spirits as his helpers. Thus, in addition to his wealth, political power, and bravery in war, he is regarded as one of the best curers in the whole Kamu Valley.

As is the case in most of the activities among the Kapauku, shamanism also has its economic aspect. For a simple cure a native practitioner is paid from 2 to 6 old Kapauku cowries. The pay, however, can only be claimed after the cure is proved to have been successful. In addition to his monetary remuneration, a shaman derives high social prestige from his activity, and many friends and admirers. He ranks second only to a prosperous *tonowi,* the rich man.

The most frequent and the most important types of white magical rites are those concerned with curing disease. After a man has been "attacked by an evil spirit which tries to remove his soul" he turns for help to a shaman. The practitioner, applying all his skill and knowledge, tries to expel the evil spirit from the body of the patient either by bribing it or by forcing it out with the help of his own guardian spirit. Almost every magical cure that I have witnessed differed from the others in individual selection of the elements of the magical rites, over-all organization of the procedure, sequence of the technique, and wording of the particular spells. The shamans also differ in their eloquence and their.knowledge of lore and the use of the various paraphernalia. However, they all make use of certain elements of magical performance that are the property of the profession. Some of the most frequently used and, therefore, important elements of curative magic follow. Every magical procedure that I have observed started with a prayer by the shaman to the sun and moon Creator and to the shaman's guardian spirits. During the performance that follows, a shaman invariably uses a magically powerful plant. Its selection often depends on the diagnosis of the cause of the disease. As a rule the evil spirits are associated with particular plants. However, the most generally used plant, often utilized next to that which a particular spirit requires, is the green variety of the *ti* plant. Its stem, with a few leaves left at its end, is a repellent of most of the evil spirits. The shaman carries it around his patient, touches the head and other parts of the body with it, shakes it furiously, and thus expels the spirit that causes the disease. Very often the plants are used together with glowing embers. The whole bundle, consisting of both ingredients, is moved counterclockwise, followed immediately by clockwise circles, around the patient's head. This performance is almost always accompanied by involved, repetitive spells, uttered rapidly by the shaman, and by his spitting on the embers as well as around the patient. Since water is believed to have a purifying force the shaman and the sick man apply it freely to different parts of their bodies. The spirits are almost always bribed by the plants and glowing embers —augmented by sacrificial small birds, rats, or intestines of some larger animals—into leaving the body of the patient. Toward the end of the rite these offerings are hung on a pole, or thrown behind the shaman into the bush. The procedure may be combined with performances during which a shaman extracts, by sleight of hand, an evil object from the patient's body. The practitioner may also try to recapture the patient's soul on the end of the *ti* plant broom and reintroduce it into the sick man's body. The magician's trance, as well as his dreams, may also be employed in the cure. Through these the shaman claims to have learned the cause of the illness as well as the remedy for it. At the end of a magical ceremony he suggests some special observances that the patient must follow as a continuation of his cure. For a period of time, or for the rest of his life, he may be ordered to refrain from eating certain species of food plants or animals. As condition for a complete recovery the patient may be requested to manifest his generosity. This consists usually of killing a pig and distributing its meat free to the public. Sometimes he may also be asked to set aside a certain quantity of cowries for his son's inheritance.

Preventive magic, which is almost the same as curative magic, is employed when a man suspects an enemy of having sent an evil spirit against him. In such a case the endangered individual does not wait until the onset of the affliction but seeks shamanistic help ahead of time.

Kego ekigai, a countermagic (lit.: "to untie sorcery") is used when a man believes himself to be a victim of sorcery. The shaman employs the curative magical procedure just described, except that the ceremony is more elaborate, the bribes more numerous, and a greater generosity is generally required from the patient. This is necessary because the evil spirit that causes the disease is not only asked to leave the body of the patient, but has to be actually bribed into attacking the sick man's enemy, the sorcerer. It stands to reason that for such an amount of work the evil spirit must be offered more than he usually gets for simply refraining from killing his victim.

Rain-stopping and rain-making rites are usually very simple, although the rain-stopping magic belongs to the "imitative" type: a tree branch may be cut and left in the house to dry, or ashes are thrown into the rain to stop it by "drying it out."

An example of magic for economic profit has been given in the description of *juwo,* the pig feast ceremony. It usually consists of an elaborate spell and an offering. Love magic, on the other hand, is a simple rite of the "contagious" type. A piece of *janebo* plant is introduced into the food of the loved person; if it is eaten, he is believed to fall helplessly in love with the individual who used the rite.

War magic is designed to help a man against arrow wounds. It may be administered either to a wounded man or it can be used as preventive magic on warriors going into battle. In either case the magic is directed against an evil spirit who is believed to enter the man's body through a wound and manifest itself through fever, infection, and agony. Kapauku believe that magic cannot be employed successfully to safeguard one from being hit by an arrow. This, as they say, depends on the skill of the archer in hitting the target and on the speed with which a man can avoid the oncoming missiles. The war-magic rite is simple, consisting of licking either *jape daagu,* a highly polished charm stone, or green branches of the *bi* tree, and rubbing them in slow motion over one's body.

Most of these magical rites are not limited to treatment of a single individual; they can be applied to a whole group of persons. In instances of group magic, many individuals are treated at the same time, and some of the rites have to be modified in order to adapt them to the different situation. The adaptation is, however, always a simple and mechanical matter. For example, in a curative magic the shaman does not move the bundle of plant material and embers around the head of every individual separately, but he circles with it around the whole group.

Kego tai, "the practice of sorcery," usually requires its own specialist *kego epi me,* "the sorcerer." Many of the attributes of a Kapauku sorcerer closely parallel those of a shaman. Like the practitioner of white magic, the sorcerer makes use of his spirit guardians and helpers, uses spells, magical plants, and offerings, and is usually a healthy, middle-aged man. However, unlike a shaman, the sorcerer possesses his own supernatural power that is believed to be independent of any spirit helper. Because of his malicious practices the status of a known sorcerer is low. He is feared and hated by most of the people, is ostracized, and is sometimes even executed by a relative of a man who is believed to have been killed by the sorcerer's practice.

The Kapauku practitioner of the black art performs his rites in secrecy; those requiring a complex ritual he executes in the bush. The rites vary in complexity from an "evil eye," accompanied by a magical formula, through contagious magic, in which a spell is cast upon something belonging to the victim (for example, a hair clipping, piece of clothing or spoor), to a complex rite of imitative magic. In the latter performance the sorcerer uses the magical plant of that evil spirit who is asked to be the sorcerer's helper in killing the prospective victim. For example, a cut *otikai* tree stem is planted in the ground, spells are uttered, and offerings are given to the *Tege,* "evil spirit," who is believed to be magically associated with the *otikai* tree. Then, with a single blow of a machete or an ax the *otikai* tree stem is cut in half. *Tege* is supposed to kill the victim magically in the same way that the tree was cut down. As in the case of white magic, sorcery also employs a plant with a general applicability in all its rites. It is *jukune,* the red variety of the *ti* plant. An incident, which testifies also to the Kapauku "sense of humor," will demonstrate the fear the people have of the black magic and its major paraphernalia, *jukune.* I once visited a mission in the Kapauku territory and was surprised to see that the church, whose walls were made of an Indonesian type of matting, were torn, and the whole nice structure damaged. It looked as if a bulldozer had gone through it. The missionary explained to me that for an unknown reason his congregation, during a service, suddenly became panicky, and tore through the walls and door in order to escape from the structure. Since the missionary had conducted services in that village for several months without any such incident, the sudden violent behavior of the people seemed to be inexplicable. Upon inquiry, I found that the Kapauku houseboy of the missionary, who also helped him with the services, as a joke had substituted *jukune* for a green variety of the *ti* plant that had been used for blessing the congregation with holy water. When the unfortunate missionary started to swing the plant associated with sorcery, the frantic congregation, in order to escape the "missionary's black magic," escaped wherever there was an opening or a weak wall in the structure.

Kapauku World View

Most of the Kapauku people do not ponder the nature of life and the universe around them. They are empiricists who are not inclined to speculate and philosophize. The topics that interest them do not concern the supernatural or metaphysics; indeed, they usually talk about such unphilosophical subjects as contemporary power relations, concrete monetary transactions, love affairs, or news concerning pig feasts and dancing. Philosophizing they leave to the few especially gifted individuals who make it their hobby to try to penetrate the nature of things beyond the barrier imposed by the human senses. Accordingly, the systematic and logically consistent philosophy that is described next is by no means the property of the Kapauku tribe as a whole; it belongs to a few very intelligent individuals from the southern part of the Kamu Valley who have elaborated their views of the universe into a logical, systematic whole. Consequently I do not want to imply that the following exposition is necessarily the belief of Kapauku in regions other than the Kamu Valley. For the ideas that follow I am especially indebted to Ijaaj Jokagaibo of Aigii, Ijaaj Kaadootajbii of Jagawaugii, Ijaaj Awiitigaaj of Botukebo, Ijaaj Amoje of Botukebo, and Ijaaj Amoje of Aigii. The first two are middle-aged, the first a prosperous headman and the second a skilled shaman, the third is an old headman of Botukebo, and the last two, now deceased, were in 1955 and 1959 the oldest men of the region.

In the view of the Kamu Kapauku the world is a flat block of stone and soil that is surrounded with water and extends indefinitely into the depth, thus providing no room for an underworld. Above the earth is a solid bowl of blue sky that limits the known world at the horizon. During the day the sun travels from east to west on the inside of the inverted bowl of sky and thus provides light. In the evening it slips under the edge of the bowl and travels above it from west to east. Because the bowl of the sky is solid, it shields the earth from the sun's rays, thus bringing night. An empirical support for this theory, according to my informants, is provided by the stars. They are thought to be perforations in the solid sky, through which the rays of the returning sun penetrate at night. In the morning the sun emerges in the east under the canopy of the sky, thus marking a new day. Beyond the solid bowl of sky exists another world that may be similar to ours, the abode of Ugatame, the Creator.

The universe itself and all existence was *ebijata,* "designed by Ugatame," the Creator, Ugatame has a dual nature: he is supposed to be masculine and feminine at the same time, is referred to as the two entities, and is manifested to the people by the duality of the sun and the moon. To my inquiry whether Ugatame was the sun and the moon I received as an answer a firm denial. Sun is conceived as a ball of fire, because it provides light and is warm; moon is believed to be a cold light like that of a firefly or the bacteria that infest rotting wood. Sun and moon are only manifestations of Ugatame who thus makes his presence known to the people. They definitely are not the Creator himself. To make the matters more complex, in the old days the people did not even have a single term for this deity. They referred to him as "sun and moon, they two." While the concept of the Creator is an old one, as evidenced by its use in many prayers and magical rites in 1954, the term "Ugatame" seems to be new, originating probably under the missionary influence in Kapauku regions that are situated east of the Kamu Valley. Ugatame is omniscient, omnipotent, and omnipresent, credited with the creation of all things and with having determined all events. Strangely enough, however, he is believed not to exist himself. When I questioned this contention, a Kapauku defended it skillfully by a question: "But how can he exist when he created all the existence?" Obviously Ugatame is beyond existence, because to the Kapauku all that exists must be of phenomenal nature; one must be able either to see, hear, smell, taste, or feel it. But Creator is beyond this phenomenal dimension, because of the simple reason that he created it. Because he is, so to speak, in the fifth dimension and is not of phenomenal nature, he is able to be omnipresent.

From this position the Kapauku "logicians" reason further that evil as well as good have been equally created and determined by Ugatame. Consequently he can be neither good, nor bad, but he must be indifferent. Evil and good to the Kapauku are always relative notions: an act may be good for one person while at the same time it is obviously harmful to someone else. In the Kapauku language *enaa* "good," and *peu,* "bad," are not substantives but only adjectives that have to be related to a subject. Thus even language reflects the Kapauku "Weltanschauung or relativity." As a further extrapolation from these premises the Kapauku argue that because everything has been determined by Ugatame there cannot be anything like a free will in man, and consequently there is no sin. After all, Creator created good as well as evil, so why should he punish a man for executing his own will? He would actually be turning against his own work. In other words in his religious philosophizing, a Kapauku is basically logical; he refuses to accept dogmas that either oppose clear empirical evidence or that contradict his common sense and logic. On this subject an incident in the year 1955 was illuminating to me. A very old man from the Mapia region, supported by his two sons, managed to come to see me in the Kamu Valley. As he explained to me, his main purpose in coming was a problem he wanted to have clarified before he died. The problem concerned the white man. He could not understand how it was possible that the white man could be so clever and ingenious in designinig such amazing contrivances as aeroplanes (which the old man could see flying over his valley), guns, medicines, clothes, and steel tools, and at the same time could be so primitive and illogical in his religion. "How can you think," he argued, "that a man can sin and can have a free will, and at the same time believe that your God is omnipotent, and that he created the world and determined all the happenings? If he determined all that happens, and (therefore) also the bad deeds, how can a man be held responsible? Why, if he is omnipotent, did the Creator have to change himself into a man and allow himself to be killed (crucified) when it would have been enough for him just to order men to behave?" The notion that anything can be absolutely bad or good was quite incomprehensible to him. Furthermore, the Christian notion of man resembling God in appearance appeared to him as utterly primitive (*tabe-tabe,* "stupid").

It was not only the deep philosophical notion of Christianity that some of these natives rejected or misinterpreted. A more concrete idea of hell and heaven, for example, elicited reactions in some of them that were certainly not desired by the missionaries. For example, Ijaaj Awiitigaaj, the headman of Botukebo, once came to me with a surprising idea. He stated flatly that if Christianity reflected the true nature of the world, then he desired to go to hell. The reason was quite obvious. In hell there was an eternal fire. What a device for a Kapauku, having a fire that burns forever and never having to bother with fuel! "In hell it must be warm and cosy," argued the old headman, "while it stands to reason that up there (in the heaven above the clouds) it must be dreadfully cold. You can feel it when you climb the high mountains how cold it must be up there." Besides the advantage of having an eternal fire, hell had at least one more strong attraction for Awiitigaaj. Since he had 10 wives, he argued, he would have to surrender 9 of them if he went into the cold heaven. On the contrary, in hell he could keep all of them and stay there happily in a warm environment.

In the world created by Ugatame everything is real to the Kapauku. Even the evil spirits that belong to the creation of Ugatame are necessarily phenomenal and not supernatural. They manifest themselves as sickness and, according to the Kapauku, their behavior follows natural laws as does that of man and animals. They belong to several well-defined types that one can compare to our notion of species. For example, Tege, the chief demon and spirit of the woods, apears in visions and dreams in which he often assumes the shape of a young man. All the spirits combine evil and good functions and have definite sex. However, their essence is immaterial. They penetrate the bodies of their victims in the same way that two shadows might fuse together. By their singular-plural existence, which I have compared to our notion of species, they are at the same time mortal and immortal, destructable and indestructible. A shaman may kill a Tege, but in its plural aspect (as a species) it continues to exist, making its appearance in the singular form in cases of sickness in other people. To the Kapauku there is little about a spirit that is supernatural. It is manifested in disease and behaves like a living organism. Consequently I had no problem in explaining our conception of disease as being the result of tiny organisms harming the body of man. "There is little difference between our and your opinion of the nature of disease," claimed a Kapauku. "We call it *enija,* 'the evil spirit,' because we cannot see it. You have glasses (*douja*) through which you see the little creatures (*jina*). You call it *jina,* and we call it *enija.* What is the difference? What both of us are actually concerned with is their manifestation, the disease." Reflecting this practical and empirical attitude toward things, Kapauku accepted wholeheartedly the European medicine with its manifested results.

Although the essence of spirits is immaterial, animals, as a contrast, are purely material beings. They are living organisms that have no spiritual counterpart, the soul. The only exceptions to this generalization are man and the dog. Both of these are believed to combine two basic components: the material and the spiritual, the body and the soul. This duality of human nature is, according to the Kapauku, empirically verifiable. Whereas there is no problem in this respect with the body, obviously one cannot see the soul of a man directly. However, its separate existence is proven to the Kapauku by the occurrence of dreams. These are believed to be the experience of the soul alone, in which the body does not participate. In dreams the soul temporarily leaves its biological repository and moves in a spiritual world, while the body rests unconsciously in one place.

The dreams, and on rare occasions the visions, reveal to the Kapauku thinker two realities: *bagume dou* (lit.: "to see a dream"), the spiritual perception, and *bagume dojogoo gai* (lit.: "thinking while dreaming"), the spiritual conception. The first reality reflects the sensual experience in a dreamlike seeing, touching, and tasting things, and hearing sounds while dreaming; the other reality consists of the thinking one does while dreaming. As a counterpart to these dream experiences stand two realities in which the man lives during the day. The first, to which the natives refer as *ani dou,* "I see," *ani juwii* "I hear," and so forth, which we may call "bodily perception"; the other is *gai* (lit.: "thinking"), which we may call "conception." Unlike perception, we cannot refer to *gai* ("thinking") as bodily conception. While my Kapauku informants claimed the body can see, feel, taste, smell, and hear independently of the soul, they asserted that the thinking process is a complex one, a combined effort of the body and the soul. A body alone cannot think. As a consequence the spiritual component in man, and also in the dog, seems in the Kapauku conceptualization to be more important than the bodily one. In this sense then, man and dog are closer to spirits than to animals.

If man has a dual nature, the spiritual and the material, the question then arises: "Who am I?" Ego is certainly not the body, because Kapauku readily argue that one can live even after losing a large part of it. Neither can Ego be *ani ipuwe enija*, "the soul," because the Kapauku actually prays to his own soul and thus dissociates it from Ego. When Ego is neither the body nor the soul, then it is obvious that to a Kapauku "I" means consciousness; it means the thinking process that is the cooperative effort of the body and the soul. Consequently for the Kapauku, as for some European philosophers, to think means to be—*"cogito ergo sum."* Thus, strictly speaking, "I" exists when I am awake. During the dream or a vision Ego ceases temporarily to function. The Kapauku term for "to live" is *umii-tou,* which actually expresses well the notions here discussed. While *umii* means to sleep, referring to the separate existence of the soul, *tou* means "to stay in place," referring to the material existence of the body. To live, *umii-tou,* suggests to the Kapauku the combination of the spiritual and bodily existence and their cooperation. "My body stays in place (*tou*), my soul dreams (*umii*) (lit.: 'sleeps') and I live (*umii-tou*)."

Whenever the cooperation of the body and the soul is impeded, Ego either ceases to function temporarily (as in a dream), or may be annihilated forever if the cessation of the cooperation is permanent (as in death). Cooperation of the soul with the body is certainly obstructed, according to the Kapauku, when the soul cannot freely determine the actions of the body. Such an obstruction to the spiritual and bodily cooperation equals an obstruction to life itself and is consequently regarded always as dangerous and often as fatal. It occurs when a man is in a coma and cannot move his body. It is also present when a man is forced against his own free will either into a performance of a task (forced labor) or if he is prevented from moving around by being tied or locked up. Because of these notions, it is claimed, Kapauku abhor the white man's jail and do not have in their cultural inventory a place for institutions such as slavery, serfdom, war captivity, imprisonment, or compulsory behavior. Personal freedom to them is essential to living. In bringing up their children Kapauku never force their offspring to do things. Punishment is always a reprimand for past wrong behavior, but never a compulsion into a behavior. A Dutch doctor became aware of this when he, with my assistance, inoculated the Kamu Kapauku against the dreadful disease, yaws. The people were well aware of the necessity and advantages of the injections and came in large numbers to my house to receive the beneficial treatment. Among the people was a man with a six-year-old boy. After the father had received his injection the doctor turned to the son. The boy, however, became frightened and refused the treatment. When the doctor tried to proceed despite the boy's objections, the father stopped him abruptly: "You heard the boy, he said no!" and "no" it was, because to the little boy's life and prosperity his freedom of decision was believed to be more essential than the treatment against the disease.

Death to the Kapauku is rather a complicated event. Basically it is a permanent separation of the body and the soul and a permanent end to their cooperation. An immediate effect of this cessation of the bodily and spiritual cooperation is the elimination of Ego. A subsequent consequence of the death is a slow decay of the body. In this respect, then, death is destructive. It causes the dissolution of Ego and the rotting away of the body. The soul, on the other hand, being a true spirit, is unaffected by death. It leaves the body and proceeds to the virgin forests and mountains where it stays during the day. The Kapauku have no clear conception about the nature of the soul. It is simply immaterial, and consequently hard to be conceived by a man. Only when pressed by questioning would they speculate and suggest that it may be a translucent image of the body. During the night the departed soul may return to the village and linger around the houses. Its relationship to the living depends upon the character of the person prior to his death, and also upon the way the body was disposed of during the funeral. If it has been given a decent burial in a structure provided with a window that allows the body "to look" toward the house of the relatives, the soul is pleased and becomes a guardian to the inhabitants of the house. It is believed to shield them especially from the attacks of evil spirits (manifested in disease). *Okai ipuwe enija,* "the soul," usually incorporates the good qualities of the deseased person. Death, however, also separates the malevolent potentialities of the individual and associates them with *tene,* the departed shadow. Despite the fact that *tene* is a spirit like the departed soul and behaves in a very similar way, it differs from the latter in its appearance and nature. Its image is an etheric, dark outline of the dead man like a detached shadow. While the *tene* does occasionally help its protegé in the same way a departed soul does, it is believed to be always motivated either by its own profit or by the harm it can do to other people. A soul is viewed as good-natured, but a departed shadow is regarded always as malevolent and is terribly feared for its sinister actions. Consequently, in white magic a man requests help from the departed souls of his relatives, while in sorcery, where killing other people is the purpose, one usually employs the services of *tene,* the departed shadow.

The difference between a soul and a departed shadow goes even farther and pertains also to the origin of the two entities. Whereas soul is a spirit that has been created by Ugatame a long time ago, and has been in existence during the life of the individual, *tene,* the departed shadow, has been created as a spirit only at the time of the individual's death. In other words, during the life of the individual *tene* did not exist. The passive shadow of a living person is not *tene,* it is called *aija,* "the shadow," and is believed to have no spiritual properties. Thus it never experiences dreams, and the Kapauku never pray to their own shadows. With the arrival of death the shadow not only automatically departs, but it also becomes an evil spirit whose nature appears to be a malevolent spiritual reflection of the soul's bad attributes. Thus death not only destroys an individual by a severence of the ties between his body and his soul, killing the former and setting free and independent the latter, but it also gives birth to a new spirit, the *tene.* Consequently, to a Kapauku death is not only a destructive force—it also creates. Because of its terrible creation of *tene* the natives have an additional reason to fear death.

5

Main Characteristics of the Kapauku Culture

KAPAUKU CULTURE exhibits many patterns that stand in sharp contrast to those of the lowland Papuans of the northern and southern coasts of West New Guinea. In many respects their culture reminds one of Western civilization. Their way of life lacks the great preoccupation with the supernatural, the ceremonies, the head hunting, and cannibalism that one invariably encounters on the coast of New Guinea. Instead of an emphasis upon such activities one finds here a stress on secularism, rationalism, and quantitative orientation, combined with a conspicuous absence of any representative art and elaborate ritual. This concluding chapter will briefly elaborate on these and a few other main characteristics of the Kapauku culture.

Throughout the earlier chapters we have encountered a strong Kapauku emphasis upon individualism. This emphasis is obviously very important for understanding the motivations, actions, and reasoning which relate to the production, distribution, and consumption of native goods. All Kapauku economic undertakings are executed primarily because, as the natives put it, *ani beu kai peu,* "I need," or "I want to do it for my own benefit." I have never heard an economic argument in which the needs of a social group have been put forward as a justification for a position taken by a discussant. Consequently, because it is always the Ego who "needs things" and who, through his effort, acquires these, it is not surprising that all commodities are owned individually, thus leaving almost no room for common property. Movables, canoes, houses, pigs, and land always have only one proprietor. Even tracts of virgin forests are claimed by individual persons. The exceptions to this pattern seem to be the barren tops of mountains and the larger streams owned by the sublineages, and small lakes that belong to lineages. Also, exceptionally, a house may be "claimed" by two owners. However, even these exceptions appear to be illusory if we investigate the matter closely. Since barren land and rock are unfit for cultivation, and water by itself has no economic value, no Kapauku is actually interested in owning these areas. However, when it comes to the animals that inhabit these places, they become individual property as soon as a man or woman catches them. What actually is "owned" by the sublineages or lineages in common is only the right of their members to acquire the animals as personal property through hunting, trapping, fishing, or collecting. In the case of a house, the two co-owners who have built it together own individually those planks and sheets of bark that they have contributed to the building. We have also seen that large structures from which a whole community profits, such as bridges, main ditches, and fences, legally speaking form conglomerations of individual ownership rights to segments of the structures.

The Kapauku idea of individual ownership applies also to food consumed within the household. At every meal in the men's dormitory there is always an individual who owns the food and functions as a host to the rest of the people. Also, all economic cooperation within the household has to be viewed from the point of individualism. When the owner of a house asks the members of his household to help with garden work, care for piglets, make canoes or planks, dig ditches, or build a house, he is actually proposing a business contract. His coresidents will be either reimbursed with shell money, food, or other commodities, or the head of the household will reciprocate the favor in the future when his coresidents need his help in turn. The result of work accomplished by the household members never becomes a common property of the whole group. It is always a single individual from this group who claims as his own the fruits of the common effort. The pattern of the native labor is also shaped according to the requirements of individualism. A Kapauku man or a woman always tends to work in such a way that his or her accomplishment can be clearly distinguished from those of the other workers. If a main drainage ditch is cut through the swampy soil of the Kamu Valley, or a main fence is erected around a large area to exclude the domestic and wild pigs, the individuals always try to construct discrete sections for which they will be responsible and which they can call their own property. If making a large garden requires the labor of several workers (male or female) the area is always divided and a worker becomes responsible only for the specific part assigned to his care.

Kapauku individualism is, of course, not limited to the realm of economics. In the native political structure it is embodied in its most important institution—*tonowi,* the rich headman. This individual becomes prominent in his group through his own effort and skill in amassing great wealth and in redistributing it cleverly among less fortunate individuals, who thus become his debtors and dependable supporters in political affairs. There are no rules according to which a man assumes leadership on the basis of heritage, election, or formal investiture by a superior. Everything depends on his individual effort and economic success. As may be expected, most of the rich political leaders are self-made men who did not inherit their fortunes. Native groups that are politically organized usually have one leader who decides the various political issues and who adjudicates legal disputes. If there are two individuals in the same group in the position of leadership, they do not act as a unified body whose consensus would settle the various problems. On the contrary, each of them acts independently in deciding a case. The allocation of jurisdiction is usually simple: it falls to the first *tonowi* who comes to the scene of the conflict. His coheadman either refrains from interference or actively supports the decision made by his colleague. Consequently the Kapauku political and legal organization has no formal councils of elders, juries, or governing bodies composed of several members. Political and legal decisions are handed down by single influential individuals who, after pronouncing their verdicts, try through rhetoric to have them accepted.

Not even war is spared from the influence of individualism. The pattern of fighting is shaped strictly along individualistic lines. There are no phalanxes, no mass action of warriors in closed ranks who try to break through the enemy's lines. On the contrary, the warriors are dispersed so that their individual success in shooting an enemy is indisputable. A victory dance identifies the successful marksman who can then claim his reward for killing an enemy. This strong singular motivation is also apparent in a group of snipers who penetrate the enemy's territory for the purpose of killing a man. Invariably a single warrior is charged with the task. While his comrades wait in hiding, he makes the final approach to the hostile village where he kills his victim from ambush. The rest of his party merely provide a cover for his exploit.

Even the Kapauku ceremonial life is strongly affected by individualism. All Kapauku ceremonies have a single man as *ipuwe*, the owner. He personally derives prestige or blame from the event. In this regard his cosponsors always have a secondary position. All the *ugaa* songs sung in the dance houses during the cycles of pig feasts are compositions of single individuals who regard them as their personal property. In the sphere of the native religion the only ceremonies that exist are those performed by the shamans. Every such performance is, of course, a solo act of a particular witchdoctor or sorcerer.

The education of the young Kapauku is geared to instill into them individualism and independence. A boy sometimes receives lessons that we might regard as brutal. It is not a rare occurrence for a father deliberately to defraud his own child to "teach him a lesson." Early in his life a boy is given a garden of his own and is encouraged to begin his financial career. Similarly, a young girl weeds and harvests a special plot assigned to her care, which is well set off from similar plots of her mother and sisters.

One of the roots of the Kapauku individualism is anchored in the native philosophy of life. The natives firmly believe that the essence of life is a free cooperation of the body and the soul. Any interference in this cooperation endangers the life of the individual. The soul (mind), when unable to control freely the actions of the body, becomes displeased, and tries to sever its relationship, thus ultimately causing death of the individual. Consequently, parents never use punishment to force a child into a certain behavior. Rather, it is a reprimand for past bad behavior. The child is never told to do things, he is always asked. In accordance with these notions the Kapauku society has no jails, servitude, slavery, or prisoners of war. All these institutions imply limitations to individual freedom that the Kapauku believe would result in death. They think it is more humane to kill an enemy who cannot run away than to capture him and let him slowly die of lack of personal freedom.

Since freedom of movement and of premeditated action is regarded as a basic condition of life it would be highly incongruous if in such conditions one encountered the same enforcement of laws and decisions that we in the West are accustomed to. Consequently the native authorities do not compel their followers by force or threat of force to comply with their decisions. They try to persuade them through oratory, or by threats of withdrawing credit or not granting future monetary, legal, or political support. In this way they preserve the people's personal independence. A follower always has a choice—either to comply with the decision of his headman and receive monetary advantages and political and legal favors, or to disregard his leader's wishes at the price of antagonizing him and being denied various favors. Thus a Kapauku is independent in the sense that all his actions follow his own decisions rather than someone else's. The concept of physical force, or the threat of it, is certainly not essential for the existence of legal control. The important thing is that the legal decisions are properly made and obeyed. The mechanism that induces such compliance differs from one society to another.

The Kapauku belief in individualism is linked with their emphasis upon the secular. As has been pointed out, Kapauku ceremonial life concerns primarily the realm of economics rather than the supernatural. The magical elements that enter into events such as a pig feast, fund-gathering ceremony, pig market, wedding, or birth ceremony, are very simple, inconspicuous, and nonessential. In many cases they might not even be missed. Not all the rich sponsors of feasts believe in the necessity of the magical performances. They openly admit that they are convinced that the success of a feast is due to their own efforts rather than to a supernatural agent. It is not surprising that the most elaborate ceremonies have to do with the native economy and profit making while the only religious ceremonies (those of a magical nature) are rather simple affairs. However, even these performances have a secular purpose such as curing a patient or killing an enemy, rather than propitiating a supernatural force. The conspicuous absence of fertility rites, group initiation, carvings and paintings of supernatural beings, and preoccupation with the dead speaks eloquently for the native secularism.

The emphasis on secularism is closely connected with the natives' rationalistic and almost scientific view of the world. The Kapauku religion is not studded with numerous rationally inexplicable dogmas that are so characteristic of some of the world's great religions. Whatever cannot be either perceived through the senses, or "logically deduced" from such perceptions, the natives reject. Their philosophy of their world and of the supernatural is always a logically consistent construct that shows few of the contradictions that we find in Western beliefs. Once the premises are given, everything else follows logically. The rationalism and scientific attitude are also apparent from the sharp native dissociation of the various realities of life. To a Kapauku what "is" (exists) has to be perceptible by the senses. Thus the supernatural does not exist, the people only believe in it. In conformance with their secularistic orientation the natives are not too interested in explaining the unknown; they hestiate to speculate. Most often they satisfy themselves with a simple statement of ignorance and a disinterested *ani ewo*, "I do not know." I have never witnessed an argument concerning purely philosophical speculations or the supernatural.

Kapauku live in a wealth- and profit-oriented society. This orientation forms a logical complement to their individualism and secularism. If one tried to assign the term "cultural focus" to a part of the Kapauku culture, without much hestitation one would have to select the combination of sweet potatoes, pigs, and shell money. These three items comprise the important components of the Kapauku process of wealth formation. Wealth to a Kapauku is almost everything that he desires and strives for during his life. It gives him economic security and comfort, offers him great prestige, and can make him a headman and a supreme judge of his group. No wonder, then, that most of the native activities are wealth oriented. Even such an unlikely enterprise as war lures many natives from neutral political confederacies to join conflicts as mercenaries. If one of these helpers succeeds in killing an enemy, the reward, called *dabe uwo*, is so great that the successful archer becomes a rich man, so to speak, overnight. A Kapauku is willing to do almost anything for money. For example, the best way to get rid of the enemy's women who, having occupied a hill behind the battle lines of the opposite side, betray the movements of the warriors by shouting advice to their husbands fighting on the other side, is to throw a few beads or cowries down the hill. Immediately these females forget the war, their husbands, as well as their mission, and run into the tall grass to collect the treasures. I have used this trick on several occasions when my adopted "sons" (there were 48 of them) became engaged in furious stick fights with other boys. As soon as a handful of my blue glass beads hit the battleground the animosity was forgotten and the combatants feverishly scrambled for the money. This native preference for profit over almost anything else was once well demonstrated by one of my adopted daughters called Peronika. She was a thirteen-year-old, very intelligent girl who cooked and kept house for me. Once a Dutch police officer visited me and we talked about the high intelligence of some of the natives. My friend, however, was very skeptical on this subject. In order to convince him that his prejudice was unfounded, I told him about the brilliance of my Peronika. Immediately he set out to test my claim. He offered her money for some silly performances which also included a mad dance that is always performed only by the Kapauku males. Peronika readily accepted the business proposition and acted as a clown as long as the beads kept coming from the officer. After he had enough proof of the girl's "silliness and naïveté" he turned to me and made a slighting remark: "and this is your clever girl." I interpreted the sentence to Peronika, with a reproach that she had let me down and had, through her buffoonery, convinced the officer that she was silly, and possibly even stupid. She laughed at me and exclaimed: "I am not so sure who is actually more stupid—I who performed the silly things or the gentleman who paid for the performance."

The profit motivation of the Kapauku has also penetrated their relationship to Christianity and missionaries. The following story has been repeated in various localities and became so notorious that even a book written on the Kapauku bears a title that captures the highlight of the story and emphasizes the people's lust for profit. People of several villages regularly visited, and obviously enjoyed, Sunday services at a missionary church. After the services were over, the kind missionary distributed to his congregation tobacco and other desirables. He was beginning to regard the people as already half-converted Christians. However, the supply of tobacco ran low and the missionary had to wait several weeks for a new shipment. A curious phenomenon accompanied these events. As the supplies and the distribution of the tobacco dwindled, the attendance of the church declined, until it stopped completely. The missionary went to the local headman to inquire into the reasons for the people's disastrous neglect of their spiritual needs. The headman explained the problem very briefly and succinctly: "No tobacco, no hallelujah."

The Kapauku emphasis on objectivity and exactness is manifest in the personality of the people by their quantitative rather than qualitative world view. Their highly developed decimal counting system enables them to count even into thousands. This skill is an indispensable tool in their money economy. To my knowledge none of the neighboring tribes can boast of anything even approaching the mathematical ability of the Kapauku. The Kapauku designed a decimal counting system that stops at 60 and starts over again, having as higher units 600 and 3600. Not only is counting used in their economic transactions, but the people show a peculiar obsession for numbers and a craving for counting. They count their wives, children, days, visitors at feasts and, of course, their shell and glass bead money. At any feast, or in the evening in the village, a visitor invariably finds groups of people squatting over strings of shell money, engaged in counting them. Thanks to this emphasis and preoccupation with quantity I was able to secure exact numerical data on trade transactions and on the wealth of the people which, in turn, enabled me to analyze the native economy quantitatively. In my contact with the people I tried to exploit their passion for counting as much as possible. For example, I often rewarded my most reliable informants as well as my best "adopted sons" by granting them permission to count my thousands of glass beads. The honored and fortunate individual often squatted over my boxes for as many as four hours. At the end of his counting he would report my wealth with a victorious smile: "You have 6722 beads in your boxes. That means that you have spent 623 beads since Gubeeni counted your money three days ago. I would suggest that you order more beads in about thirty days so that you do not run out of funds." This financial finding would later be pronounced publicly in front of my house to a multitude of less fortunate informants and boys. Afterward, the report and the rate of my spending provided a topic for discussion which sometimes lasted long into the night. My finances have never been in better order than during my stay among the Kapauku.

The quantitative orientation of the people leads them into placing value upon higher numbers and larger volume. Accordingly, a tall individual is admired and a weak or small one is regarded as *peu,* bad. The name for a small child up to seven years of age is *peujoka,* which literally means "a bad child." Most of the objects that are small are bad, or at least not so good as larger ones. The people's obsession with quantity often assumes forms that come as a shock to a Western observer. Once I received a magazine with a cover portrait of a beautiful, smiling girl. I showed it to my Papuan friends and expected an outburst of enthusiasm over the girl's appearance and also, possibly, some sexual jokes. To my great surprise the natives failed completely to react to the girl's beauty. Instead they started to count her teeth! Their reactions to other pictures were similar. In a picture of a large American city they counted all the cars in the streets and the windows of the numerous skyscrapers. A Navy carrier was considered to be a most rewarding sight because of a large number of airplanes on its deck. Similarly, a picture of a crowd of spectators watching a football match proved to be a great success. On the other hand, the dour face of Mr. Malenkov, with nothing to count, proved to be a complete failure.

The Kapauku logical and quantitatively conceived universe is relativistic. There are no absolute values detached from their relativistic context. Since all that happens has been determined by the Creator, there cannot be sin, and there is also no concept of anything that is absolutely bad or absolutely good. As has been shown, the native words *enaa,* good, and *peu,* bad, are adjectives rather than substantives. There is no word in the native vocabulary that could be translated as "the evil," or "the goodness." Bad and good are only relative ideas that have to be used in a concrete context. Thus the question: "Is killing a man good or bad?" elicits surprise and confusion on the part of a Kapauku. After hesitating, he asks: "Killing of which man?" and, "Good for whom?" Naturally, killing a man is good for his enemies and bad for his relatives and friends. One can imagine the difficulties the Christian missionaries have when they try to convey to these people the basic tenets of Western religion and philosophy.

6

The First Two Decades of Exposure to Civilization

A Methodological Imperative and Short History of Contact

THE TRUE NATURE of all social phenomena, and therefore also those forming tribal Kapauku culture, are dynamic in nature. Accordingly, culture change and the onset of the process of acculturation do not imply a disturbance of any structural equilibrium that is supposed to be "normal" to a society. Actually such an equilibrium would be highly abnormal. It has always been my contention that static models of societies are unrealistic, especially those created by members of the functionalist and structuralist schools of social anthropology. Sociocultural change need not be explained apart from the structure of a society—it should be part of it. As a consequence, when I first went to study the Stone-Age Kapauku it was my intention to return several times and to make this society the subject of a long-term research in order to record properly the cyclical, repetitive, and one-directional changes in the observed behavior of the people and in their ideas, values, and attitudes.

Soon after my research began it became obvious that Kapauku society was not undergoing only one-directional slow change of an evolutionary nature, but also that cycles of several years' duration were affecting the native life profoundly. To observe just a segment of these cycles would have invited distortion. For example, the ecological situation and agricultural picture change in a cycle of fourteen to sixteen years because the land must lie fallow for this time before it can be cultivated again without suffering lasting damage. And it is particularly important to understand that the Kapauku pig feast is repeated in a given lineage approximately once in six years. A study of this society the first year after such a feast, or the last year before it, would yield radically different results that might adversely affect an economic interpretation because of the different size of the pig population and the scope of sweet potato cultivation (the pigs are fattened by these tubers), trade patterns, and consumption.

There has been, of course, another and perhaps the most important reason for my long-term research. I wanted to study the first decade of the peoples' contact with the civilized world. I wanted to witness the changes which a Stone-Age culture undergoes in adjustment to the modern world of steel and atomic energy. During my first research in 1954–1955 the Kapauku of the Kamu Valley were not yet "pacified" and exposed to colonial rule, so I had a rare opportunity to study a tribal people in their truly aboriginal condition. As a matter of fact the governor of what then was known as Netherlands New Guinea, Dr. Jan Van Baal (himself a well-known anthropologist), promised that as long as I stayed in the Kamu Valley the region would not be brought under the government's administrative control. Thus only after my departure in 1955 did the acculturation process begin to affect Kapauku culture. Consequently, unlike many anthropologists I did not follow governmental forces into pacified areas. In 1955 I saw civilization approach the Kamu Valley from the outside and shared the native curiosity, fears, apprehension, and their interest in learning from technologically superior strangers. I had no need to reconstruct a "zero level of acculturation," and during my three subsequent research periods (1959, 1962, 1975) I could study the changes as they occurred. In this way I avoided the danger of circular reasoning by which an anthropologist studies the present and modified culture of a people, reconstructing the old unadulterated stage which in turn he uses to interpret the changes that accounted for the existence of the present modified culture. Indeed this prolonged study of the process of acculturation has been my main reason for planning a systematic and periodic restudy of the people. Unfortunately, political changes after 1962 prevented me from continuing my planned visits every three years, and I could not resume my program until 1975. In spite of these problems the changes were recorded by my "formal best friend" and my Kapauku "adopted" sons (48) and daughters (4) who during my absence functioned as competent and accurate field workers, reporting the changes and supplying me by post during my absence and orally when I returned with a wealth of case material. In this chapter I shall discuss some of the highlights of the Kamu Kapauku history of exposure to the blessings as well as drawbacks of modern civilization during the last twenty years.

I will conclude this introductory statement by a brief survey of the important historical events that have marked the recent Kapauku history of contact with Western and Indonesian civilizations. The first confrontation the Kapauku had with the civilized world was a dramatic one. In 1936 a small plane, the first the natives had ever seen, appeared above Paniai Lake, spreading terror among them, especially the women who were fishing from their dugout canoes. Many of them dove overboard to escape the flying monster. It was piloted by Lieutenant F. J. Wissel. News of this event spread all over the Kapauku territory. It was such a shock that after twenty years almost all my informants in the Kamu Valley could still describe the circumstances under which they first learned of this incredible event. This episode was so well imprinted in their memories that I could use it as a historical point for determining peoples' ages— they could tell me how old they were at that memorable time by pointing out a child or an adolescent whose age corresponded to theirs at the time of Lt. Wissel's flight. In 1938 the Dutch created a government outpost at Enarotali on Lake Paniai, which they had soon to abandon because of the Japanese advance into the New Guinea area during World War II. In 1946 the Dutch Administration returned to reopen the outpost at the lake. Their influence and pacification spread from there to a few neighboring valleys and to two lakes to the south, Tage and Tigi. Such was the situation when I arrived in 1954 in the Kamu Valley, a region of still virgin cultural heritage.

When I reflect upon my early days in New Guinea and my appearance in the valley I must conclude that my arrival produced another shock for the local people. I remember vividly how many of them were frightened by my appearance, until I recognized its cause—my clothing. Afterwards I wore only shorts, thus showing the natives that in spite of my equipment and strange hair and skin color I was as human as they were. Nevertheless they did not accept this fact immediately or completely. They told me that I was immortal because of my white skin. They argued that their crayfish were white when young, then gradually darkened and finally shed their carapaces, thus becoming rejuvenated and starting a new cycle. I argued against this by pointing out that they never gave a crayfish a chance to die of a natural cause, and that white men die of old age as a crayfish does, only they must give both of us a chance. Unfortunately my arguments were weakened because of the unfortunate circumstances that I tan very well; my skin exposed to the tropical sun became bronze and finally dark brown. My intellectual adversaries jubilantly pointed out my changed appearance as paralleling that of a growing crayfish—our skins darkened. And they predicted: "And now you will shed your skin and become pink again." True enough, I peeled—the hot New Guinea sun was too much for me. So I lost the argument on empirical grounds. On the other hand, I got friendly acceptance from many of the natives who came to me and laughed and pointed out that I had much in common with human beings, which meant of course with the Kapauku. Like some of them I lied socially in order to keep the appearance of equality. A truly moral rich Kapauku always denies that he is rich or greater in any way than other tribesmen. Similarly, I was supposed to have lied, and claimed not to be immortal, in order to pretend equality with the mortal Kapauku.

As this episode indicates, my influence upon the Kapauku during my first research in 1954–1955 was limited to the sphere of new ideas, some of them necessarily inaccurate. Most of the ideas and information about the outer civilized world were offered by myself to the Kamu Valley natives during the last "moon" of my stay, as it was originally agreed upon my arrival in the valley. I explained truthfully my role as an anthropolgist and my intention to learn their language and culture and write books about them. In order that I learn properly and that people not be influenced by my ideas, we agreed that the roles of student and teacher would be reversed only during the last moon when they could question me on any subject they chose. And so the agreement was kept with a few exceptions. I had to tell the natives some things about myself and my family. For example, I had to disclose that I was already married and discuss with them our custom of monogamy in order to avoid problems arising from my refusal to marry some of the local girls. In addition to enriching their knowledge, I caused a small monetary inflation with blue glass beads which I gave as payment for food, gifts, and services; my total expenditure of these beads was carefully calculated in my quantitative analysis of the Kapauku economy. I also distributed a few axes, knives, machetes, and items of clothing, all of which the people refused for exchange purposes and accepted only as gifts.

After my departure in 1955 the Kamu Valley became pacified by the Dutch colonial police, wars were prohibited, and serious legal disputes involving violence (especially manslaughter) were referred to the newly installed administration officer who established his residence at Moanemani, on the western edge of the large Kamu Valley. A Catholic mission school was built in Botukebo, the village of my intensive quantitative research, and an Indonesian catechist and his wife took over the task of instruction. Thus the Kamu people were introduced to state power and Christianity at the same time. Prior to my departure in 1955 I made several recommendations to the Dutch Administration, one of which asked for abolition of the practice of jailing offenders and substituting adequate fines. By that time the region was controlled, and the Kapauku resented jail as an inhuman and degrading institution. In accordance with their belief, as we have seen, a man deprived of his personal independence of action and liberty is doomed, his soul eventually leaves him, and he dies. Thus thieves and other small offenders were, in their eyes, punished by slow death resulting from even a jail sentence of a few months. I predicted an early uprising should abolition of jail as well as a few other less important recommendations be rejected. Indeed, one year later the Kapauku revolted and after bloody fighting were defeated and pacified. After this uprising a new and rather extraordinary nativistic movement called *Wege bagee* stimulated the inhabitants of the southern part of the Kamu Valley to build two new villages on the mountain slopes. They incorporated in them some elements from Western civilization, including a well-defined village plan, flower beds, and a remarkable sanitation system characterized by latrines, exclusion of pigs from the village, and elimination of the proverbial New Guinea mud by thorough drainage of the premises.

A further major historical event took place in 1958 when the Dutch Administration built an airstrip at the village of Moanemani and established direct communication between the Kamu Valley and the outside world. Thus within only five years a Stone-Age Papuan society, whose many members had not previously seen a white man, had been brought into the atomic age and confronted with such modern inventions as airplanes, cars, guns, radio, cameras, and modern medicine.

Of what they saw of Western civilization, the Kapauku really valued most its technology and economic system. The pronounced individualism of Western capitalism was highly appreciated. The Kapauku exploited the economic possibilities offered to them by the pacification of the wide area, formerly dangerous and inaccessible to their trade adventures. They began to conduct trade expeditions by land as well as by air. Indeed, some of the bolder entrepreneurs chartered their own planes for business expeditions to distant regions. The Kapauku spread all over the civilized parts of West New Guinea so that in 1962 I had no difficulty in communicating with local natives in many places because I could always find a bilingual Kapauku trader or employee of the Dutch Administration or of the various missions who gladly (for a fee of course) could serve as an interpreter of my Kapauku speech into the local language.

The year 1962 marked the end of an era for New Guinea. The Dutch government withdrew, yielding the territory to Indonesia. The Kapauku were disappointed because they believed, as they had been told, that the Dutch were to set them free. Change to the Indonesian administration went smoothly through an intervening brief administration by the United Nations. The Indonesians faced problems similar to those that confronted the Dutch. The Kapauku simply wanted to be free and independent. Moreover, they expected the new administrators, who were regarded as rich, to share their wealth through loans and *jegeka*—prolonged loans—with the people. Opposition to the new rule culminated in a second revolt which proved to be at least as bloody as the first one. As in the first insurrection the Kapauku were not united, the people of Tigi Lake siding with the administration while the natives of the Kamu Valley as a whole joined the Paniai people on the opposition side. I suffered a personal loss when one of my adopted sons, Ijaaj Wijaagowode, was shot and killed in one of the engagements. The outcome of the hostilities for the Kamu Valley was not a defeat but a reasonable compromise. Indonesia has kept the region under control by an Indonesian district officer, a very decent and understanding man, while the police force, composed of uniformed Kapauku, keeps peace and order in the valley.

Pacification—Change in Political Structure

When a colonial power moves into a new territory it inevitably effects immediate profound changes in the native political structure. "Pacification" usually means not only establishing peace by preventing war between tribes or smaller autonomous political units, it also implies elimination of independence and limitation or complete abrogation of the powers of the native political leadership. By establishing itself as a government over a formerly politically segmented territory, it converts external conflicts into internal disputes which are dealt with and adjudicated peacefully by courts of the new colonial administration. Furthermore, it almost always takes away from the native chiefs their jurisdiction over grave criminal offenses, thus no longer allowing them to impose the sanctions of death or maiming. As a result, their political functions are either severely curtailed or are completely obliterated and replaced by a new native system of controls subordinated to the colonial government of which it forms the lowest executive (and sometimes also judicial) level.

The pacified Kamu Valley was no exception to these generalizations. The elimination of native warfare, which was endemic in this region, deprived the Kapauku political confederacies of one of their major functions. Interconfederational disputes, which formerly were solved by either diplomatic negotiations or war, began to be referred to the court of the Dutch civil administration at Moanemani in the Kamu Valley; serious criminal offenses were brought to the attention of the district officer at Enarotali and, later, at Waghete in the Tigi Lake regions. As a consequence, political ties which formerly had so closely bound Kapauku lineages into confederacies, began to loosen, and the lineages and their constituent villages became more independent.

The prestige and position of the traditional Kapauku headman was certainly undermined. However, the last real blow to the *tonowi* was dealt unwittingly by the Dutch Administration when it built an airstrip at Moanemani. As shown above in the discussion of credit (p. 27), the availability of ready cash to the young Kapauku men ended their dependence on loans from the rich headmen, which in turn caused the latter to lose their influence and prestige. The old political structure was thus doomed. However, not all the headmen suffered political collapse. Actually, as a response to the white man's administration and a challenge to it, the influence of a few leaders of the former political confederacies began to spread beyond the old and now vanishing political boundaries. Because of the degrees of acculturation of the various groups, new alliances were formed and new antagonisms originated. Thus, while the old type of confederacy leadership declined beyond recognition even as soon as 1959, leaders of some of the newly formed broader alliances assumed unprecented regionwide influence. As a result, in 1962 the Kamu Valley was divided roughly into two politically opposed segments. One, having as its center the village of Moanemani, seat of the Dutch administrator, comprised roughly the western and northwestern part of the valley. It included the villages of Mauwa, Pouja, Moanemani, Degeidide, Obajo, Ugapuga, and Gimouda. The other, which united several formerly hostile political confederacies, comprised the eastern and southern parts of the valley, including the lineages of the former Ijaaj-Pigome confederacy (the object of my intensive and quantitative research) and "our" former archenemies—the Waine-Tibaakoto confederacy. So it happened that a Tibaakoto headman, who in 1955 promised to kill me as one of his major enemies (I was considered a wealthy member of the Ijaaj-Pigome confederacy), became the father-in-law of one of my adopted sons in 1962 and therefore my in-law relative. I had to give him most of the beautifully large cowry shells I had bought in Tahiti, as partial payment of his daughter's bride price. Similarly, all over the Kamu Valley, former traditional enemies were united into new alliances which divided the valley into two politically hostile camps. The western and northwestern political union boasted of friendship of the Dutch administrative officer at Moanemani, while the southern and eastern half stood in opposition. This division, however, never resulted in open violence, and conflicts were confined to the courts, where the two camps always supported their constituents. The speaker and leader of the southern and eastern part of the valley was my "best Kapauku friend" Jokagaibo, who thus slowly assumed an informal leadership of this new political conglomerate.

With the advent of the Indonesian Administration the political situation in the Kamu changed slightly—only to the extent that the valley was assigned its own district officer, who continued to reside in Moanemani. He is a congenial young man who does his best in a difficult situation. He lives with his family in a small new house and has his office nearby. The old residence of the

Dutch administrator disintegrated as did my house in Itoda. However, in other districts there has been a more radical change: in Waghete of the Tigi Lake region and in Enarotali on Lake Paniai, native Kapauku have been assigned as district officers! Furthermore, the old Kapauku territory has been incorporated by the Indonesian Administration, as one of sixteen districts, into a region called Paniai, presided over by a Resident Officer (*bupati*) whose headquarters are located in the coastal town of Nabire on Geelvink Bay.

Nabire, which counted about 300 people when I visited it in 1962, in 1975 boasted of 15,000 inhabitants, mostly from Java, but also including about 2,000 Kapauku who arrived from the interior. Some 52 of them are employed by the administration as officials while the rest work in the local lumber and building industries and in other odd jobs. Most of these have not relinquished the Kapauku urge to farm, and they cultivate their own gardens in their free time, aided by their families. The Kapauku women sell their surplus farm produce to Indonesians at the local covered market every day from six to eight o'clock in the morning. The town is now connected with the Kamu Valley (Moanemani) by a dirt road which is still being developed while parts of it are steadily overgrowing with jungle. Nonetheless this connector, no matter how imperfect at the moment, constitutes a great improvement over the former isolation of the interior of West New Guinea (Irian Jaya). At present, however, the only effective connection with the Kapauku of the interior is still by planes which land on several of the airstrips in the tribe's territory.

With respect to the informal native political structure, the Indonesians have initiated another important change. As an aftermath of the uprisings and the new political alignments in the Kamu Valley, a few of the formerly important headmen have emerged as an informal body of political leaders of the valley as discussed above. They are often called upon to deal with the formal Indonesian administration and represent the "Kapauku point of view"; and among themselves they settle less important disputes which do not involve serious violence.

This history of changes in political structures has been closely related to a radical transformation in the native law and administration of justice. Already in 1959 the rules governing jurisdiction, as well as those pertaining to criminal and civil law, had changed profoundly from the time of my first investigation. It was most interesting for me to record the skillful administration of justice by the Dutch officers who interpreted native law and tried to reconcile it with the canons of justice of Western civilization. Usually cases of serious violence were taken up *ex officio* by the Dutch officer at Moanemani, while nonviolent disputes were adjudicated only if the parties to the dispute themselves arrived at the administrator's residence and requested a decision. Very often these requests came in cases where the litigants belonged to two formerly independent confederacies. Only later, after the development of the wider leadership in the valley, were these trouble cases solved by the few headmen who had enlarged their jurisdiction beyond the former political boundaries.

In 1959, while visiting the Dutch courts in session, I was amused to see my book *Kapauku Papuans and Their Law* being used by the administrative officer as a legal codex—as "the source of Kapauku law." Although I was amused, this was certainly not the reaction of all the Kapauku; as a matter of fact, my work was very unpopular with some of them for an obvious reason. My book dealt with law as it was administered within the Ijaaj-Pigome confederacy of the southern part of the Kamu Valley. Traditionally, every such political confederacy had a different legal system and there were sixteen of them in the Kamu Valley alone. So what was actually happening was that the Dutch officer, by using my book for all cases brought to his attention, unwittingly promoted the legal system of one political confederacy to a sort of "tribal law," which had never existed before. So the amused people were, of course, all my Ijaaj-Pigome confederates, who joked about it or even poked fun at the other Kapauku. One, tongue in cheek, even threatened them: "if you fellows are not going to behave we shall make our American big shot (Amerikaibo) write another and even tougher book." Of course, I could not see such injustice being done and stopped the practice by explaining the situation to the surprised Dutch official. "My God," he exclaimed, "and I thought these guys were just stubborn and obnoxious."

The Indonesian Administration has changed the legal situation to such an extent that cases of murder and insurrection are referred nowadays to the professional judge at Nabire, while other legal cases are settled by the Kapauku police of the Kamu Valley in a less formal way.

All these political and legal changes have not, of course, been accomplished without problems for both the administration and the tribes. The problems, if taken one by one, appear to be rather insignificant, save for a few exceptions. However, their accumulation provided the cause for the two bloody uprisings in which both sides suffered loss of lives. The administrators meant well; often they thought they acted in the interest of the other side. However, this did not always work out as was intended. The administration provided legal adjudication in an area where formerly only diplomatic negotiations and wars had prevailed. It was often not realized that the natives preferred violence or war to the limitation of their freedom. The civilized administrators thought that beating up a fellow, wounding him with an arrow shot into his thigh, or executing him were far harsher punishments than serving a jail sentence while working in a civilized community. Indeed they reasoned that the individual could learn many important skills in prison. Kapauku thought otherwise. Jail was an inhuman punishment, and forced labor an action unworthy of human beings; they preferred fines, wounding, or death.

Other problems arose because of well-intended public works from which the native population would benefit. An obvious case was the building of roads. Before any development of a civilized life can be attempted in any area brought under state control, there must be safe and efficient communication. To traverse any distance in Kapauku territory had always meant to wade through treacherous swamps, walk through mud, slide on slick roots in the jungle, balance oneself on a pole over a crevice that was often tens of yards deep. Indeed I have a picture of one of my expeditions when we had to cross a stream on a "bridge" (two thin and flexible poles both submerged under more than three feet of water). People have been known to drown on some of the "roads" through swamps. So building a road would obviously benefit everyone. To this effect the Dutch Administration decided to build the roads, provide the natives with necessary tools and equipment, and even pay the workers a reasonable amount of money for which they could buy what they wished in the government store. In the beginning there seems to have been some enthusiasm, which dwindled very fast. Finally the concerned official had trouble getting people to work even for higher wages.

Exasperated by broken promises and the lack of labor, the official sent out native police to forcibly round up recalcitrant workers from the various communities. Bobii Ipouga of Tadauto was bound and taken by police to their outpost in spite of the fact, as Kapauku informants claimed, that their community had already sent twelve people to build the roads. Later three additional men, with hands bound, were sent to do the work. The Debei Valley people sent a deputation to me with their objections. One of the headmen complained bitterly: "I was taught Christianity by the American people. They claimed that one should love other people and that violence and killing is bad. However the white man is violating his principles whenever it is profitable to him. It seems that Christianity should be good only for the Kapauku." Since the Dutch district official was a good man who most likely did not know what the zealous police were doing behind his back, I wrote him a letter in which I deplored forced labor and stated that during the war in Czechoslovakia we were also forced by the Nazis to work, and received good pay but that none of us was happy about it. The situation was swiftly corrected. Of course, there remained the problem of how to make the Kapauku work and enjoy it. So I made a bet with the Dutch officer. If he provided the tools, the Kamu Valley Kapauku would build the road for free. The bet was accepted (one bottle of champagne), we received the tools, and I held several public lectures about the importance of good and safe communication. To be more convincing I showed the people pictures from *Life* magazine with roads, highways, and bridges. They were impressed, and held a meeting at which they decided to build a road system in the Kamu Valley.

A deputation came to me to announce the good news. Then they asked me how much would I pay a worker. I exclaimed in surprise and then screaming, as a good Kapauku orator should do, I explained that I was an American, that New Guinea was not my country, that the road would be theirs and not mine, that they would profit from it and use it while I would have to return to America. Indeed, I cried, they should pay me for my advice and negotiating for the tools. The Kapauku were first astonished, then they burst into laughter, pummeling each other with their fists in joy: "You are really quite a guy, you are now like a Kapauku. You know when to give and when to refuse a nonsense!" And so it was, no pay on either side. They worked, I criticized, and here and there treated the workers to meals and some goodies from the government shop which had to survive a three-day trip from Paniai Lake. The road construction proceeded well and swiftly and connected four villages of our confederacy: Botukebo, Kojogeepa, Obajbegaa, and Notiito. It traversed several swamps and climbed a low hill. The reason for the success was not, of course, my lectures. It was the fact that Kapauku could do it themselves. It was *their* road and they employed a very different system of management in its construction. Instead of communal labor and a commonly owned facility, the new road, like their main drainage ditch, was owned individually: each segment of it that traversed somebody's property was owned, worked upon, and cared for by the owner of the land. The road was thus communal only in the sense that all people could use it.

When I returned in 1962 "our road" was still standing and well cared for, while some of the government roads had suffered from neglect. This example beautifully demonstrates that industrial countries should help but never impose a development in the emerging nations. Such imposition, no matter how well meant and planned, is doomed to failure if it incorporates ideas basically foreign and antagonistic to the dominant principles of the native culture. As we cannot induce some of the communally minded old American Indian tribes to accept capitalist attitudes and enterprises, the state could not make out of an individualistic and ideally egalitarian Kapauku a communally minded socialist who would accept projects planned and directed by an often unwieldy bureaucracy. For this reason the advice of an objective anthropologist, who has done his research properly, who speaks the native language, and who is not burdened by adherence to any such sociopolitical creeds as capitalism, Marxism, or any other nineteenth-century isms, should be invaluable to a public administrator.

Legal Change in Incest Prohibition—a Field Experiment

In addition to enabling social phenomena to be viewed in their true, dynamic nature, long-term research offers many other benefits. One of the most important is the opportunity it provides the field worker to construct hypotheses concerning the causal relationships of social phenomena, predict resulting future change, and verify the prediction at a later field session. Thus a social scientist may come very close to laboratory experimentation, but in his case the experiment is designed by history rather than the researcher. Social sciences have been called "soft" sciences because it is claimed that they are unable to predict—and prediction constitutes the heuristic value of science. Long-term research can correct this situation.

Such an opportunity was offered to me in 1955 when I recorded a dramatic modification of the laws of incest among the people of the Ijaaj-Pigome confederacy and the resulting changes in the social structure of the Botukebo community. The legal change was initiated by Awiitigaaj, the headman of the Ijaaj-Enona sublineage, and it was possible to record the pertinent history and motivations of the headmen, as well as the attitudes of the Papuans toward the innovation. I published these data in an article in 1958 and, on the basis of my analysis of quantitative data on the internationalization of the new laws of incest, I also included specific predictions of changes which were to follow. Upon my return in 1959 I verified my prediction, administered further attitude internalization tests, made new predictions, and again summarized the results in a paper presented to the Annual Meeting of the American Anthropological Association in Philadelphia in 1961. When I went to New Guinea again in 1962 I tested my theory on sociopolitical change and checked the specific predictions

I had made in 1961. Details of this example of research in culture dynamics and the testing of hypotheses in long-term research situations follow.

The legal change affecting the regulation of incest started in about 1935. At that time the influential young headman Awiitigaaj fell in love with his beautiful third paternal parallel cousin, who unfortunately belonged to his own sib. Kapauku law is very explicit about marriages within the sib: it prohibits them under penalty of death. Nonetheless, Awiitigaaj did not hesitate to break the taboo and elope with the girl. Outraged relatives pursued the couple. The girl's father Ugataga, who was a co-headman of the Ijaaj-Jamaina sublineage and lived in the neighboring village of Kojogepa, ruled that his daughter and her lover be shot to death by arrows as Kapauku customary law demanded. His verdict was accepted by the headman of the whole Ijaaj-Pigome confederacy as justified. To Awiitigaaj, a man well versed in native law and political intrigue, this dangerous situation came as a challenge. Together with his beautiful cousin he hid in the depths of the nearby forest, assuming that the girl's father would soon realize the futility of the pursuit and in time, after his temper calmed down, might be willing to drop the charges, forego the punishment, and accept a lucrative bride price. Awiitigaaj calculated that Ugataga, clever businessman and politician that he was, would see the disadvantage of killing his own daughter and thus forfeiting a bride price. By upholding traditional law he would end with no daughter and no money—a very hard prospect for even a very moral Kapauku. Awiitigaaj speculated, and correctly, that Ugataga would show great anger in public and conduct an exhausting search in the forest until he tired out the patrilineal relatives and bored the other tribesmen. If he eventually gave up the pursuit and accepted the inevitable, he would preserve the public's high opinion of his morality, the life of his daughter, and the prospect of an unusually large bride price. The acceptance of bride price would make the marriage formally valid and would legally absolve him. Awiitigaaj's analysis of the situation and predictions of the developments were marvelously accurate, which some of our skeptics in predicting human behavior should notice. Ugataga performed as anticipated. Awiitigaaj's maternal relatives, acting as go-betweens, asked his paternal relatives for the bride price. Legally speaking, this act implicitly recognized the incestuous marriage and Awiitigaaj stepped into Kapauku sociolegal history as a great innovator, a man who successfully broke a law against incest anod remained unpunished.

However, this was not the end of the incident. Awiitigaaj, as a headman himself, could ill afford to be regarded as a violator of law. Consequently, to clothe his action with an air of legality, he promulgated a new law which stated that it was permissible to marry within a sib so long as the couple were at least second cousins. In public he defended his new piece of so-called legislation by ingeniously constructing sociopolitical arguments. Privately he confessed to me that he broke the taboo simply because he was in love with the girl. Thus his case, supported by his arguments about a new and more sensible law, became a precedent which brought about a far-reaching change in the law and social structure of the Ijaaj-Pigome confederacy. Awiitigaaj himself married three additional second paternal parallel cousins, and he was followed by many men in the confederacy. Thus by 1954, 19 "incestuous marriages" were contracted in the studied political unit (6.44 of all marriages contracted between 1935 and 1954). In the same year when I administered an internalization test (attitude and popularity tests) I found that 57.5 percent of the Botukebo people accepted, 37.5 rejected, and 5 percent were indifferent to the new law. However, the acceptance of the new rule spread from Awiitigaaj's sublineage to the rest of the units of the Ijaaj-Pigome confederacy, and affected those to different degrees. Consequently, the law of incest in the confederacy became complicated and, to a casual observer, bewildering. In the Ijaaj-Enona sublineage marriages between second paternal parallel cousins became permissible, but in the rest of the related Ijaaj sublineages and in the Ijaaj-Notiito lineage only a marriage between third paternal parallel cousins, and preferably between those who came from different sublineages, was regarded as legal. Moreover, all these rules stood in sharp contrast to the law of the Pigome and Dou lineages, the other constituent group members of the confederacy. Pigome intrasib marriages remained prohibited and were punishable by severe beatings, while in the Dou lineage, execution was still the legal mandate. Thus the law of incest in the Ijaaj-Pigome political confederacy became complex and understandable only if individual cases and decisions were linked to the particular subgroups of that political union.

Unfortunately, Awiitigaaj did not leave matters as they were. He noticed that half the intrasib marriages in the confederacy were concluded between partners not only of the same lineage but also of the same village of Botukebo. His political genius and his need to establish his incestuous legal innovation on a more convincing moral basis seized upon this new trend toward village endogamy. Because of prestige, and to refute the incessant criticisms and charges of immorality directed at him by his domestic opposition and external enemy, he decided to render his new incest law more convincing by making it more formal and complex. He drew a line through the Botukebo community and divided it into two halves. The line was so drawn that in each half of the village resided members of his Enona sublineage who were related only as far as first cousins. Awiitigaaj named the two halves *wejato* and *auwejato*, proclaiming them to be exogamous moieties (halves) and spoke in favor of marrying across these lines. In his legislative enthusiasm he went ever farther and advocated a new and revolutionary village plan. The scattered conglomeration of the traditional Kapauku settlement was to be abandoned and a lineal village plan adopted, in which the houses would stand in a single compact row that was divided in the middle by a gap. This gap would symbolize the incest boundary and each of the moieties was to co-occupy one-half of the row. Marriages concluded within the village of Botukebo were supposed to occur only across this line. On the basis of a test of internalization of the new law and the new residential scheme, I predicted in 1955 that Awiitigaaj's new housing pattern would succeed, that the increased endogamy would enhance the position of women (the married women who married into Botukebo would no longer be outsiders), and that fewer marriages would occur across the political confederacy line, thus increasing the likelihood of more wars.

The pacification of the Kamu Valley by the Dutch in 1956 prevented the test of the last hypothesis. However, when I returned in 1959 and first saw Botukebo from the higher Debei Valley, I was shocked to see that my prediction of the new village plan had come true. Below the slope lay Botukebo, consisting of a single compact row of houses, divided by a gap in the middle. In front of the houses was a main path with a large drainage ditch to keep it dry. Although I was pleased that my prediction was correct, I cannot say that I was completely happy. I was frightened by the knowledge that we could predict human behavior. I do not think that we Westerners actually like it, although we certainly strive for it. We still emotionally embrace the idea of free human will, free from any compulsion, be it only cultural.

Having dealt with the history of the legislative changes, we shall now inquire into the reasons for the social acceptance of these unprecedented innovations. First, to be sure, we must dispose of an idea, proposed by Sir Edmund Leach, that the division of Botukebo into moieties had anything to do with a normal process of fission. Fission, which in this case means segmentation of groups of the Kapauku society, does occur but not along incest lines, because the whole sib remains exogamous. Fission does not create new sibs but new lineages, which then move into and occupy another virgin territory, retaining the old incest taboos. Botukebo did not split and drift apart—on the contrary it was even more firmly cemented together by the new intracommunity marriage system!

Elsewhere, abolition of the rules of exogamy was often caused by severe depopulation. This was certainly not the case in Botukebo. Its population actually increased. Lowie (1920:157–162) and Murdock (1949:137) advanced several hypotheses for causes of the abolition of exogamy. These had to do with changes in food production, types of residence, and rules of inheritance. However, these possibilities can also be dismissed because none of these changes occurred in the confederacy. The same patterns of food production, residence, and inheritance prevailed as in all other Kapauku confederacies, none of which underwent changes leading to abolition of the rule of sib exogamy and creation of residential moiety groups within the villages. In my original article of 1958 I suggested the cause for the acceptance of Awiitigaaj's innovation. I claimed that it was political in nature. Members of the Ijaaj and Pigome lineages were latecomers into the Kamu Valley. Approximately 140 years ago, after natural drainage had made the flat Kamu Valley habitable and fit for cultivation, people who lived on the edges of the valley slowly moved in, occupying the new and fertile land. This was, however, not the case with the Ijaaj people who emigrated from the Mapia region, and the Pigome lineage whose members came from the vicinity of the Lake Paniai. Unlike the rest of the occupants of the new territory, they were immigrants into the region and surrounded by hostile neighbors. Inevitably, conflicts arose and the Ijaaj-Pigome confederacy was intermittently embroiled in wars. Marriage in this situation presented a grave problem. Because the Ijaaj men far outnumbered their small Pigome and Dou lineage allies, in order to comply with the rules of sib exogamy they had to marry the daughters of their hostile neighbors. In time of war these wives proved to be of questionable loyalty. Many of them betrayed the war plans of their husbands to the enemy—their fathers and brothers. Indeed, some deserted their spouses. Even worse, of 11 wars during the 20 years preceding my initial research in 1954, 5 were fought because of the desertion of women from hostile confederacies whose relatives then refused to refund the bride price.

Marriages within a confederacy, in contrast, have been secure because law and order have been enforced by the headmen. Consequently, an intraconfederacy, and therefore also an intrasib marriage, eliminates a cause of war and eventual economic loss. In case of divorce, a full return of the bride price is legally guaranteed. Therefore, because of the political and marital problems, sib endogamy appeared to be the logical answer to this particular political situation. This interpretation of the reason for the acceptance of Awiitigaaj's "'legislation" is further supported by the fact that the Pigome and Dou people, who found enough wives in the much more numerous Ijaaj lineages, firmly maintained the traditional rules of exogamy and were utterly disinterested in the legislative products of Awiitigaaj's legal genius.

When the area was pacified by the Dutch in 1956, marriages all over the Kamu Valley became secure; they could not result in wars and did not put the wives' loyalty on trial. Thus if my hypothesis concerning the cause of the change of law of incest was correct, its acceptance by the people would have lessened. Because of pacification there was no longer a problem of marrying outside one's political unit. Indeed, my test of popularity of Awiitigaaj's legislation revealed in 1959 (three years after pacification) that 55.32 percent of adult and adolescent males of the Ijaaj-Enona lineage opposed the innovation and regarded it as unjustified and even immoral. An additional 2.12 percent offered no opinion, 10.64 percent gave Awiitigaaj's legislation qualified support, and only 31.91 percent of the males fully supported the abolition of sib exogamy at that time.

After the study of 1959 I predicted again, on the basis of my field data, that if the pacification of the Kamu Valley continued, sib exogamy would again be emphasized, the Botukebo village plan would revert to an irregular pattern, and the moiety system, created by Awiitigaaj, would be abolished (Pospisil 1961). In my reasoning, although the former aspects of Awiitigaaj's innovation would logically disintegrate as an immediate reaction to the failing popularity, the law itself would persist longer because the leaders themselves (Awiitigaaj, the Ijaaj-Enona headman, Ijaaj Jokagaibo, the Ijaaj Jamaina leader, and Ijaaj Ekajewaijokaipouga, head of the whole confederacy) all contracted intrasib marriages. They could hardly tolerate having their marriages pronounced illegal and themselves branded as immoral. The vested interest of the several leaders would thus keep the intrasib marriages permissible as long as these leaders kept their status, in spite of the adverse opinion of their followers.

My predicted changes of 1961 were found to be a reality upon my return to New Guinea in 1962. Because of the pacification of the valley, and the stubborn support of the abolition of the taboo on intrasib marriages by the leaders and their immediate close kin and friends, the opinions of the natives with regard to the desirability and morality of the abolition of the role of sib exogamy became sharply defined and divided. My tests disclosed that the category of people with no opinion and those of qualified support of the legal change of 1959 had completely vanished in 1962: only 34.14 percent of the people gave unqualified support to Awiitigaaj's changes (certainly a loss from 42.55 percent of support qualified and unqualified in 1959). In contrast, 65.86 percent of adolescent and adult males opposed Awiitigaaj on the abolition of the incest taboo. Of course, they could not prevail against the policy of their leaders, especially because the Dutch Administration was not at all interested in this issue. In contrast to the persistence of the official recognition of the intrasib marriages as legal, the former adjuncts of Awiitigaaj's legislation disintegrated very rapidly indeed. Since these formalistic trimmings were not regarded by Awiitigaaj as important, he did not resist decomposition of the moiety system. His lineal village plan of Botukebo reverted again to a loose conglomeration of houses without any plan whatsoever.

The inception of the Indonesian administration and the Catholic missionaries, both dedicated to eradicate "superstitions" and primitiveness from Kapauku life, certainly could not be expected to support a law upholding sib exogamy. While the Catholic missionaries might succeed in destroying the idea that intrasib marriages are incestuous by proclaiming it an outmoded pagan observance, the Indonesian government officials and police would certainly abolish the death penalty for the violation of intrasib marriage. Indeed, they would arrest the executioners as murderers. Consequently I could predict that there would again be a reversal in the history of the abolition of this incest law. However, this time it would not be a consequence of Awiitigaaj's legislative change but of the advance of civilization.

This example of legal change studied in a long-term research project shows not only that social science can predict, and that expenditure of time and funds for an extended time is justified on several grounds, but also that study of the actions of individuals in a "primitive" society is highly desirable and also imperative in order to elucidate the nature of historical processes and culture change. These are often glossed over by generalities or by hypothesizing some often mystical social forces, and expressed in convenient Durkheimian jargon.

Wege bagee—the Crazy People

The reaction of the Kapauku to the stress and strains of acculturation has not always been dismay or resistance. Actually, Western individualism and entrepreneurship appealed to them considerably. They could appreciate Western technology, which they did not regard as mystical or supernatural but as clever achievement. Since the greatest prestige in their culture can be secured through economic success rather than headhunting or prowess in war, Christianity was found to be quite compatible with their philosophical orientation, save possible for the prescription of monogamy. Because of these values and attitudes toward Western newcomers it is not surprising that when a nativistic movement sprang up, as it did in many places in New Guinea, it did not resemble the irrational cargo cult, so widesperad in the eastern part of the island. Although the members of this movement called themselves *Wege bagee,* or better, *Dimi beu bagee,* which means crazy people (*lit.:* people without thought), except for a few strange observations stemming from misinterpretation, the tenets and program were quite progressive, adaptive, and rational.

The founder of this movement was Pakage Amoje, also known as Zacharias, of Kokabaja in the Tigi Lake district. In World War II he attached himself to the Dutch district officer Victor de Bruijn and went with him to Australia. Later he became a Protestant teacher, but became antagonized to the white man to the point that he proclaimed himself district officer, burned the houses of some native adversaries, and even planned to kill a missionary. His outbursts were judged criminal by the Dutch Administration and later as symptoms of insanity, and after a term in jail, he was committed to an institution in Hollandia (now called Jayapura). After his release he was influenced by the Seventh Day Adventists and became a convinced pacifist. He began to preach the end of the world, love for thy neighbor, tolerance for the enemy, and aversion to violence. "Even if somebody comes intending to kill people, one should take it with resignation" was one of the major commandments of the movement. While preaching his belief, Pakage distributed gifts to his followers who were supposed to walk weaponless, tend their fields, be very industrious, and reject all temptation to crime, especially the widespread predilection to theft. In return for such a moral life they were supposed to be saved in the coming end of the world—they would go straight to *Ugatame* (God), while the infidels were to carry luggage for eternity, as the porters for the white man had to do.

When I came back to the Kamu Valley in 1959 the *Wege bagee* movement was in full swing. Their members had built two new communities called Obadoba and Idabagata on the slopes of the southeastern part of the valley. As so often in my research in New Guinea, I was very lucky with respect to this movement. One of my adopted sons, Tibaakoto Tibaajpouga of Mogokotu (whom I named Johannes to honor one of my anthropology friends) became the leader of the Kamu Valley chapter of the movement. Thus I had good access to the two communities and to valuable data and insight provided by Tibaakoto and his followers.

In the Kamu Valley the movement took on a very rational form. Although the religious beliefs were discussed and preaching was important, including the observation of Sunday (*Daa naago*—"tabooed day"), the secular and economic aspects of the movement were especially emphasized. The members built the new communities in large fenced-in areas which their pigs were not allowed to enter—they were provided with special stalls and had to roam outside the enclosure. The enclosed area was subject to intensive complex cultivation, which uses the familiar mounds (as described in the chapter on economy). Thus the two villages were uncommonly clean and devoid of the notorious New Guinea mud. Moreover, the people copied my outhouse in building a communal latrine; to utilize the structure to its full capacity they even planted beans on its walls so that the occupants could inspect the harvest while on the premises. Cleanliness was much emphasized. The people washed in the evening and in the morning as I used to do, and shaved or plucked their beards; and they wore clothing (if they could afford it) which they kept scrupulously clean. Their hair was washed and combed. The communities were wonderfully landscaped and even provided with beds of flowers (marigolds mostly), the seeds for which the people obtained from the missionaries. Furthermore, to my amazement I discovered that they had planted a large field with coffee trees received from the Dutch Administration, and that they were also growing many other European vegetables and cultigens.

They had rejected the old cowrie shell money and used exclusively the blue glass beads (introduced to the Kamu by myself in 1954) and Dutch paper money. For enjoyment they constructed a sand-covered soccer field on which the master of the chapter functioned as coach in the late afternoons and on Sundays. He had learned to play soccer in 1955 as a member of my soccer team which had beaten the teams of other lineages. Soccer was thus one of my early contributions to the native culture. In the game we modified some of the unattractive European regulations and ruled out prohibitions against "out" and "foul" which made the game less interesting. To kick one's opponent in the buttocks with the upper part of a bare foot was as enjoyable and harmless as kicking the ball. Because of their peaceful bias, the *Wege bagee* dropped this innovation of our team and re-established the rule against "foul." My final surprise came when they asked me to give them a lecture on the planting and cultivation of European crops. After I had delivered the speech I was paid with several chickens! Originally the Kapauku never paid anyone for speeches. When they saw my surprise they said that among them it was a general practice to pay speakers, and that they remembered that I was paid for lectures to my students in America. Several of my boys, who accompanied me but who themselves were not members of the movement, proudly carried the chickens to our home in Itoda, displaying with pride my professional earnings to the passersby. Subsequently, whenever our household was out of meat, they urged me to deliver more speeches to the *Wege bagee*.

Population Pressure, Ecology, and Economy

During my first research it was officially estimated that there were about 45,000 Kapauku, living either in territories already under Dutch control or in regions not yet pacified or even explored. Although my estimate was a little higher, it was certainly true that much of the Kapauku tribal land remained virgin and uninhabited. Nevertheless, even in those days there were areas, especially around the lakes and in the river valleys, with some concentration of population. The Kamu Valley represented a unique feature in the native ecology: a partially dried-out lake bed with exposed rich soil, especially in the northern and southeastern areas. Population density was quite high there and many villages, separated from each other by less than two kilometers, counted more than 180 inhabitants. However, even with this density there was no lack of land, and the swidden agricultural cycle could securely allow the land to lie fallow for periods of 14 to 16 years, adequate for the recuperation of the soil and restoration of the original vegetation. The population increase, although significant, was certainly not alarming. It was effectively checked by endemic warfare, disease, and especially child mortality. A woman who planned to have 6 adult children had to give birth at least to 10 on the average. With the advent of the white man, and later the Indonesians, all this changed. Elimination of warfare saved the lives of adult males, and this change came almost over night. Modern medicine checked many diseases, such as pneumonia and bacillary dysentery, both formerly the major killers of children and the old. Once a horribly crippling disease, yaws (or frambesia), a tropical, highly contagious syphilislike affliction, was completely wiped out by penicillin. The disappearance of yaws was a marvel. While witnessing it I realized many of the advantages civilized people enjoy.

Ever since I first came to New Guinea I have witnessed the concern of the medical authorities for the danger of introducing new decimating diseases into the native populations. Tuberculosis was especially feared. In the fifties whooping cough ravaged the Paniai area, and in the seventies tapeworm (*Taenia solium*) was introduced with a new strain of pigs. This has become what is now regarded as the worst affliction in the area. The people are not only hosts to this horrible worm, which lives in the colon, but unlike Europeans, are also hosts to its larvae. These enter the digestive tract with contaminated food, penetrate the blood stream, and form abscesses not only in the muscles, but what is dreadful and lethal, also in the brain, causing severe seizures, comparable to epilepsy. During such seizures many Kapauku fall into their fires and sustain horrible burns. To check the parasite in the native situation is virtually impossible short of exterminating the pig population or enforcing a strict hygiene (washing of hands, toilets, etc.).

In spite of the new disease, the Kamu Valley, and especially its northern and southern ends, had experienced almost catastrophic population increase. For example, my intensively studied Botukebo community, which in 1955 and still in 1962 had only 180 inhabitants, boasted 272 residents in 1975. Moreover, many additional Botukebans had moved to other villages or to the coastal towns. This represents an increase of about 50 percent only in residents. With all the immigrants counted it comes close to 57 percent, and that in a period of only 13 years.

The increase of population in the Kamu Valley is already reflected ecologically. Jewei Mountain has lost all of its virgin tropical forest, and there are only some remnants of forest on Pouja Mountain. Nevertheless in the southern part of the valley the ecological situation has not yet become critical; indeed it has actually improved in spite of the population increase. The reason is to be found in a radical improvement in utilization of the terrain, introduced by the Kapauku themselves upon advice from the Catholic mission. I had suggested a similar project back in 1959. A large-scale drainage of the entire Botukebo, Kojogeepa, and Jagawaugii area by large drainage ditches was undertaken, so that the periodic flooding of the valley floor was eliminated, even when torrential rains lasted several days. As a consequence, a major shift in the traditional agricultural pattern (as described in the chapter on economy) took place: the whole of the valley floor could now be utilized for intensive complex cultivation (mounding technique) to produce an unprecedented surplus of sweet potatoes and other edibles. Swidden cultivation on the slopes of the Kemuge Mountain was almost abandoned, which formerly would have been judged as highly unwise, if not outright folly. The old men still worry: "There may come sometime a really huge flood, and what happens then? We shall all starve, as old stories tell us." However, save for such a flood, the draining of the area will certainly have proved a blessing.

The willingness of the Kapauku to experiment with inventions and ideas made them very receptive to the introduction of new crops, animals, and tools. My early experimentation in 1954 with various food plants interested my friends, and some of the introduced crops, especially maize and string beans, became a great success. Chili peppers, onions, manioc, and Irish potatoes had already spread from the Paniai region into Kamu before my first research. My introduction of tomatoes was an initial success in the sense that they grew wonderfully in the damp soil of my garden. However, the Kapauku did not like the red fruit and preferred to nibble only on a few green tomatoes as appetizers. An incident made the tomato a favorite crop of the young people, however, for reasons other than its nutritional value. My boys, the 48 adopted sons, liked to play games, of which a war game fought with mudballs was a favorite. However, sometimes a stone somehow found its way into the muddy projectile, causing injury to a player. Such an incident always marred the game, resulting sometimes in a real quarrel or even a fist fight. Once when the boys were engaged in a mudball fight they hit me by accident. As I stood in my garden I grabbed the first ammunition that came to hand, a large overripe tomato, and retaliated with great success; the fruit disintegrated with a beautiful splash against the forehead of the offender. The young men screamed with excitement and joy. The tomato was certainly superior to a mudball, more spectacular, less painful, and especially no chance of cheating with a stone. So the tomato became a war game plant. Needless to say, my tomatoes soon disappeared. As a compensation the surrounding area of my house, including the nearby bush and forest, flourished with tomato plants—one aftermath of the numerous fruit battles.

A plant of major importance, introduced after my research, was coffee. First planted by the "crazy people" movement, it spread because of the financial profit it brings, and in 1975 I was treated to an excellent cup of Kamu coffee in the house of the Indonesian district officer. With the rising world prices of coffee since 1976 and 1977, the Kapauku might well have chosen the best crop available for cash income. Of course, in their 1975 economy the sweet potato was still the major capital-producing crop because of its value as fodder for pigs. Sweet potatoes then still amounted to almost 90 percent of the total cultivated area, as was the case in 1954.

In addition to food plants, agriculture also produces cultigens that provide narcotic effects. Tobacco had spread into the interior of New Guinea in the nineteenth century. Kapauku smoke pipes made of bamboo sections, and cigarettes of folded pandanus leaves, sometimes two yards long. They carry these cigarettes coiled in their net bags and puff on them whenever the occasion arises. They were disappointed that I was not a smoker. I assured them that many

Americans smoked and some of them forty or more cigarettes a day! They were astounded—the best of their smokers could not manage more than two Kapauku cigarettes a day! When I arrived in 1976 I found that many Kapauku had begun to chew betel nut from the areca palm, a custom learned from the coastal people. Areca palm, called *bau*, grows in the Kamu and the chewing habit was easily introduced.

Agriculture of the Kamu Valley may yet get a further significant boost. At Moanemani an expert agronomist from Germany is working on the particular problems of the area and on a possible further development and utilization of the now barren swamps, which contain deep humus and a wealth of organic material.

In food production the greatest help from the Western world to the Kapauku economy came in the field of animal husbandry. In 1954 the natives had already profited from the Dutch presence at the three large lakes; chickens spread from there into the territory. Toward the end of their stay the Dutch tried to introduce goats and sheep. In 1975 I found both kinds of animals privately owned by many of the Kapauku, who had received most of the beasts from the Catholic mission. The priest at Moanemani has a small ranch in his parish on which he raises cattle. So far he has not distributed any animals to the natives because of some problems with the fodder. In the western Kamu Valley, because of a lack of calcium in the soil, the quality of grass is so poor that the cattle suffered rickets. Until this problem can be solved distribution of cattle to the natives has to be postponed. There are also four horses owned by the mission and used as beasts of burden. As was mentioned above, the experiment to improve the breeding of pigs by introducing European varieties proved to be a disaster with the introduction of the tapeworm. In spite of this problem, the Kapauku economy is still pig-oriented, and the pig is the main asset to the household and the principal source of wealth.

Considerable success has been achieved with the introduction of small animals in the Kamu. Distribution of the white Wyandotte chicken has provided the natives with a bird which not only lays enough eggs but is especially heavy in meat. The objective of Kapauku chicken-raising is the bird itself rather than the eggs. Introduced ducks and geese have flourished and found a true paradise in the valley swamps. Rabbits, especially the huge Belgian varieties, are kept nowadays by many of the Kapauku. There seems to be little danger that they will become a pest, at least not in the Kamu Valley where they have little chance to escape their masters and go wild. Upon my arrival in 1975 I was given a huge white rabbit as an "arrival present" by my friend Jokagaibo after we had agreed that a pig, because of the parasites, would not be appropriate as in the old days.

As far as technology is concerned, there has been little qualitative change since my early research time. True, axes, knives, and machetes are in wide use. Pots and pans are now favored in trade because of the health problems—the missions as well as the government emphasize thorough cooking of pork to prevent the spread of the tapeworm. More people these days wear clothes, although the government's attempt to abolish the penis sheath has not met with much

The main street of Botukebo, Kamu Valley, showing the lineal village plan introduced by Awiitigaaj.

The native Kapauku policeman taking off his clothes as a punishment in front of the Dutch district officer, Den Hahn. A large group of natives are watching the policeman being discharged from his post.

Kapauku boys working on a government road to Botukebo.

A group of natives dressed in white man's clothes in front of a modern type of building at Obadoba, habitat of members of the nativistic movement—Wege bagee.

A close-up of the public latrine at Obadoba, with a view of the main village fences, sweet potato gardens, part of the Kamu Valley, and in the background the central part of Jewei Mountain.

Kapauku Papuans from Botukebo village at work on their road without the assistance of the Dutch.

success in the interior of the island. One reason is the cost of clothing and another is the problem of keeping them clean.

There has been one other major change in the food-production pattern of the Kapauku, resulting from the introduction of fish into the rivers and lakes of their territory. The immediate effect was a radical reduction of the crayfish population, a major source of proteins for many communities in the old days. Women nowadays catch fish in their nets instead of crayfish. "They had to change the way and be much quicker than before," I was assured by an informant. Generally the women use nets, especially in times of flood when one drives the fish toward a line of fisherwomen waiting with nets. Otherwise the fish are taken by hook and line, both of which are bought from the mission in the Kamu Valley. Interestingly enough, the hook, a new artifact in the Kapauku culture, is called *keipo*—the Kapauku word for needle.

A profound and rather unexpected adaptation of the Kapauku to Western and Indonesian civilizations occurred in the economic sphere. The individualistic and profit-oriented Kapauku exploited the new economic possibilities offered after pacification by the introduction of a capitalistic economy to such a degree that even the most optimistic administrator was astonished. First, the Kapauku traded with the administrative officials and missionaries, supplying them with food and labor. Soon the governmental and mission outposts were becoming dependent on the native produce. For example, the Kapauku people, because their valley lies at a lower elevation and is therefore warmer and in some areas is very fertile, regularly supplied Enarotali on Lake Paniai, the largest government settlement, with vegetables, three kinds of bananas, ginger, and very delicious limes. Indeed, in 1959 I myself was asked by several white households to arrange a more regular trade in these commodities. Second, the Kapauku traders, now protected by the colonial law, could conduct trade expeditions by land as well as by air to far-lying parts of the island. The trade flourished, not only with the whites but also with other native tribes of New Guinea. The Muju people of the southern lowlands were especially favored trade partners because, as the Kapauku claimed, they were as "business-oriented and money-concerned as we are." Business with them always proved profitable. Indeed, the enthusiasm for new trade possibilities went as far as the natives chartering their own planes for expeditions to distant regions. Dogopija Okaitobii from Waghete (Tigi Lake district) chartered at least four times in 1961–1962 a bush plane to such large towns and cities as Biak, Hollandia (nowadays Jayapura), Merauke, and to the country of the Muju. He trades in pigs, cowries, machetes, axes, clothes, and other items. Of course he learned easily and well the use of civilized currencies. In 1962 when I needed a plane, a group of Kapauku entrepreneurs allowed me to fly with them for a fee. When I found myself in the back of the Cessna bush plane with some pigs, I argued for a place next to the pilot so that I could take movies of the terrain during the flight. My transfer to the front seat was very cordially arranged—of course for an additional fee.

As I have already stated, in 1962 one could find Kapauku tradesmen and employees in any place in New Guinea—at airports, in shops, among the police, in missions, and in the government offices. For the first time I could feel at home at any of these places because I always could find a Kapauku who was willing to interpret for me.

The proliferation of employment opportunities and trade also had an effect that every economist would expect: a large influx of cash into the Kapauku economy (in terms of formerly Dutch and now Indonesian money), and a resulting inflation. Nevertheless, even in 1975 the Kapauku used their old cowries. Strangely enough this currency did not lose value over the years. Five pounds of pork (*kado*) cost in 1954 one *bomoje* type of cowrie shell. In 1959–1962 and 1975 one cowrie of this old type would still on the average buy the same amount of pork. However, the introduced blue beads which were exchanged in 1954 at the rate of 30 for one cowrie sank in value so that in 1959 a cowrie cost 60 beads, in 1962 300 beads, and in 1975 beads went out of use altogether. Large items such as a house or a canoe were selling (in terms of the stable cowrie currency) for twice as much in 1962 and 1975 as in 1954 and 1959! In contrast, the price of a steel ax, a machete, and a native net bag remained unchanged. The most devastating inflation occurred with respect to bride price. Whereas in 1954 an average amount asked for a bride would be 120 old cowries, 120 new cowries, 300 beads, 3 *dedege* (Nassarius shell) necklaces and 1 large pig, in 1959 the price went up to 120 old cowries, 360 introduced cowries, 1,800 glass beads (or more), 2 to 3 pigs, 2 large strings of tiny glass beads, 2 *dedege* necklaces, 120 Dutch guilders, and some dishes, knives, machetes, and axes. In 1975 the average bride price has become almost astronomical for a young Kapauku: 300 old cowries, 600,000 rupees (!), 5 pigs, sometimes even a sewing machine (or a typewriter!), 10 or 20 pants or shirts, 2 blankets, 5 pots, 1 or 2 machetes and an equal number of axes, and neither glass beads nor *dedege* shell necklaces were acceptable. In spite of these stiff increases in the value of brides, some individuals boasted more wives than ever. My best friend Jokagaibo probably set a record in this respect, apparently being happily married to thirteen wives!

Educated and Urbanized Kapauku

The story of culture change and acculturation would not be complete without discussing those Kapauku who left their tribal home and settled in urban environments on the coast. These migrants often combined two qualities: They were young and at least partially educated. So the first attribute to help a Kapauku in the urban environment is education. Without at least a rudimentary knowledge of reading, writing, and the use of money the natives in a town do not have much chance to succeed.

The elementary education of the people is obtained from schools founded and administered by Franciscan missionaries. In the southern Kamu Valley the first school was built in Botukebo. After the Indonesians took over the government, the school was moved to the neighboring Pueta and another one opened at Moanemani, which is now the seat of the priest who administers church affairs in the Kamu Valley. In the elementary school, which the students usually attend for four years, they are taught by a catechist teacher reading, writing, arithmetic, the Indonesian language, singing, religion, penmanship, drawing, elementary agriculture, some geography, physical hygiene, physical education, and games. Kapauku children are generally very clever at mathematics. I witnessed a test administered to forty students of the elementary school in Botukebo. It consisted of 15 mathematical problems and the results were amazing. All excepting one little girl received a full 10 points from the teacher. In all sincerity I must say that the results of this education are far superior to those of some public grade and high schools in the United States. Indeed, there it is inconceivable, as seems not to be a rarity in our country, that a student could graduate from an elementary school (not to mention high school) without a good knowledge of writing and reading. Indeed, even their knowledge of mathematics and the Indonesian language is very good after these four years. Those children who are especially good students continue in high school in Enarotali. Some of the graduates of high school go on to college, university, or the Catholic seminary at Jayapura. In 1975 I met a Kapauku college student in Nabire. He was from Waghete, and spoke both Indonesian and English fluently. We discussed a variety of topics including Kapauku culture, world history, and politics. I must say that I was impressed. After their graduation from grade or high school, Kapauku girls and women receive a useful education in what we can call home economics from the Catholic nuns. They are taught hygiene, cooking, sewing, washing, ironing, cleaning, and baby care. In this trade school they make clothes for themselves from cloth bought at wholesale from pooled funds.

The Kapauku continue to learn, and eagerly so, after they leave school. If they migrate to an urban environment their interest is in trade or office work. Some become skilled artisans, others work in the lumber and the building industry, in road building, and making fields out of the bush. In Nabire, the capital of the Paniai region (of which the Kapauku tribal territory is a part), over 2000 Kapauku live in several neighborhoods consisting of clusters of houses and gardens scattered throughout the city of 15,000. On the average they earn about 10,000 rupees per month (equals $25.00) which they augment by income from their garden produce. Of course their houses are their own so there is no rent to be paid.

One of my adopted sons, Marius (Kapauku name: Ijaaj Akaawoogi of Obajbegaa), who married my adopted daughter Antonia (Waine Amaadii of Kegegadi), left the Kamu Valley after 1962 and went to Nabire on the coast. There he and his wife were employed by the Catholic mission. Later he learned carpentry and found employment in the building industry run by the Indonesian administration. He works there from seven in the morning to one or two o'clock in the afternoon, six days a week, and earns slightly more than the average wage of 10,000 rupees per month. Antonia works from seven in the morning until two P.M. and earns about 8000 rupees. She cooks and tends the household of the Catholic pastor. After work the two are busy in five of their gardens (about eight hectares total) where they grow sweet potatoes, manioc, taro, green amaranth (a spinachlike herb), bananas, sugar cane, papaya, chili peppers, cucumbers, pole beans, coconuts, peanuts, onions, squash maize and limes; and they told me they will also start some orange trees. The fields not only provide them and their four children with food but also with a large surplus which Antonia sells at the local market every morning from six to seven o'clock usually earning between 300 and 600 rupees a day. The buyers are usually Indonesians and local Melanesians.

Our Kapauku couple, like most of their fellow tribesmen, buy only such utter necessities as clothes, margarine, and fish. They have chickens, ducks, and three dogs, but no pigs. In addition to all this activity Marius holds a third position—he does odd jobs around the parish, for which he earns 30 to 40 rupees a week. His family lives in a house which he built himself of wooden boards, receiving the galvanized iron roofing from the Indonesian government. For entertainment Marius together with other Kapauku go on expeditions, especially at night, in the tropical rain forest where they collect crayfish and hunt pythons and marsupials. On one of these hunts Marius and his friends were attacked by a crocodile, an animal they had never seen before since there are no crocodiles in the highlands. They managed to escape, loosing their lantern in the flight. With the money earned from their enterprises and multiple employment Marius buys tools and Antonia purchased a flat iron and a sewing machine. With part of the money they save they buy gifts for relatives in their home country, which they distribute when they visit them (especially Antonia) by plane. Most of the Kapauku of Nabire lead a similar life, holding second jobs, being thrifty, industrious, and trying to accumulate capital.

The Kapauku of the town of Nabire have become different from the Kapauku who remained in tribal territory, in more respects than in acquisition of additional knowledge and skills. There are as skilled carpenters as Marius in the Kamu Valley; they may even speak Indonesian as well as Marius does, but there is a basic difference between them. The Nabire Kapauku have acquired a different set of values which profoundly affect their interpersonal relationships. Our Kamu Valley Kapauku, who might also be a skilled carpenter and bilingual, regards his wife, his parents, and his children in the same way that his father and grandfather did. Indeed, his attitudes toward and relations with his wife, his son, and his daughter are similar to those his grandfather had vis-a-vis the same type of his relatives, prior to my appearance in the Kamu. In short, in the Kamu Valley the culture change seems to have been superficial, affecting technology, agriculture, animal husbandy, and political and even residential groups, but not affecting the deeper values of interpersonal networks and liaisons. In contrast, a Nabire Kapauku regards his wife as a very close life-partner indeed. She is no longer "only a wife" with his primary attachment and loyalties being directed to his parents, siblings, and children, as is the case in the tribal area. She is no longer a person who might get a divorce tomorrow and disappear with another lover, and then, if everything goes well, for whom a compensation will be paid, which the abandoned husband will use as bride price for another girl who he hopes will be more faithful than the first one. The bond between a wife and husband in Nabire becomes stronger and I would dare say primary. In complementary fashion the urban individual's relation with his brothers, father, paternal parallel cousins, and maternal relatives becomes weaker and more distant. I do not have space to discuss the causes for these differences, but I want to register their nature. It seems that the rural Kamu Kapauku and the urban Nabire Kapauku have changed in different ways. In the Kamu the form, function, nature, and in some cases the very existence of the various groups have been effected; in Nabire the personal relationships have undergone radical change. Whereas in the Kamu the confederacies disintegrated, group leadership altered, lineages lost their primacy, and villages which formerly were not groups in the social sense, became political units with a new leadership based on the model of Indonesian communities, in Nabire the relationships with the various kinsmen, friends, trade partners, and acquaintances underwent radical transformation. In terms of our prior dual analysis of the Kapauku social organization, we may say that in the Kamu Valley the change affected what we termed "societal structure" (the structure of the relationship of the segments of the society and the nature of the groups); in the town of Nabire the Ego-centered relationship or, as I have termed it, the "social structure," was radically altered. These changes can be compared with the results of my other long-term research among the peasants of the Tirol of Austria. There, as among the urban Kapauku of Nabire, the interpersonal relationships of the Tiroleans exposed to city life changed, and the Ego-centered social organization underwent radical restructuring. In contrast, however, the Tirolean groups (family, household, community, various economic and religious associations) remained untouched by their exposure to tourism and by full participation in the market economy of the nearby city of Innsbruck. From the two studies I tentatively conclude that in the Kapauku case we deal with two different processes: with *acculturation,* which affects primarily the societal structure (as exemplified by the situation in the Kamu Valley), and with *urbanization,* which alters primarily the Ego-centered social structure (as exemplified by the situation in the town of Nabire). In the Tirol we deal with only one process, that of urbanization of the peasants, the changes in which have the same structural propensities as those we find affecting the Kapauku of the urban community of Nabire. Thus my research among the primitive Kapauku, when compared with that conducted among the civilized Austrians, sheds light upon the processes of acculturation and urbanization, and allows a hypothetical differentiation between the two on the basis of their structure. The two concepts appear to be very useful; they point out basic structural differences of the two types of culture change, and they have empirical validity in cross-cultural research.

References Cited

POLANYI, KARL, CONRAD M. ARENSBERG, and HARRY W. PEARSON, *Trade and Market in Early Empires: Economics in History and Theory.* Glencoe, Illinois: Free Press, 1957.

POSPISIL, LEOPOLD, *Kapauku Papuans and Their Law* (see Recommended Reading list), 1958a.

——, 1958b, *Kapauku Papuan Political Structure* (see Recommended Reading list).

——, 1960, *The Kapauku Papuans and Their Kinship Organization* (see Recommended Reading list).

Recommended Reading

BARRAU, JACQUES, Subsistence Agriculture in Melanesia. Honolulu: *Bernice P. Bishop Museum Bulletin* 219, 1958.

A comprehensive account of agriculture in Melanesia and New Guinea.

BERNDT, RONALD M., *Excess and Restraint.* Chicago: The University of Chicago Press, 1962.

A detailed report on social control among the Kamano, Fore, Usurufa, and Jate people of the Eastern Highlands of New Guinea.

BROWN, PAULA AND M. C. BROOKFIELD, Chimbu Land and Society. *Oceania,* 30: 1–75, 1959.

A brief survey of the major institutions of the Chimbu Society of the Eastern Highlands of New Guinea.

DOBLE, MARION, *Kapauku-Malayan-Dutch-English Dictionary.* The Hague: Martinus Nijhoff, 1960.

A dictionary of about 2000 Kapauku words.

LOGCHEM, J. TH. VAN, *Gegevans Omṭrent de Socio-Politische Organisatie der Kapauku's.* Hollandia: mimeographed report, 1959.

A sketchy description of social and political organization among the Kapauku of the Paniai Lake region.

MEGGITT, M. J., The Enga of the New Guinea Highlands: Some Preliminary Observations. *Oceania,* 28:253-330, 1958.

A brief description of the social, political, and economic institutions of the Mae Enga people of the Australian part of the New Guinea Highlands.

NILLES, J., The Kuman of the Chimbu Region, Central Highlands, New Guinea. *Oceania,* 21:25-65, 1950.

A preliminary report on investigation among the Kuman Papuans of the Australian part of the New Guinea Highlands.

POSPISIL, LEOPOLD, Kapauku Papuans and Their Law. New Haven: *Yale University Publications in Anthropology*, 54, 1958.

An outline of the Kapauku culture with a detailed quantitative analysis of their law. The book is concluded with a comparative theory of law.

————, Kapauku Papuan Political Structure. In *Systems of Political Control and Bureaucracy in Human Societies*, edited by Verne F. Ray. Seattle: Proceedings of the 1958 Annual Spring Meeting of the American Ethnological Society, 9–22, 1958.

A concise outline of the Kapauku social and political institutions.

————, Social Change and Primitive Law: Consequences of a Papuan Legal Case. *American Anthropologist*, 60:832–837, 1958.

A story of a headman who through volitional action changed the Kapauku law of incest and thus brought about important changes in the native social structure.

————, The Kapauku Papuans and Their Kinship Organization. *Oceania*, 30: 188–205, 1960.

A survey of the Kapauku kinship organization and a componential analysis of their kinship terminology.

————, Kapauku Papuan Economy. New Haven: *Yale University Publications in Anthropology* 67, in press, 1963.

A detailed quantitative analysis of the technology, food quest, and economy of a Kapauku community.

READ, K. E., The Gahuku-Gama of the Central Highlands. *South Pacific*, 5, 1951.

A brief survey of the Gahuku-Gama culture of the Eastern Central Highlands of New Guinea.

REAY, M., *The Kuma, Freedom and Conformity in the New Guinea Highlands*. Melbourne: Melbourne University Press, 1959.

An account of the Kuma society with a special emphasis on social and political structure.

Glossary

AFFINAL RELATIVES: Kinsmen whose relationship to Ego has to be traced through at least one marital link.

BILATERAL: A nonunilineal principle of descent by which all consanguineal relatives are recognized.

BILATERAL SOCIETY: A society that lacks any type of unilineal kinship groups, which possesses kin groups whose membership is based exclusively upon bilateral descent.

CHATTELS: Commodities of economic value.

COLLATERAL RELATIVES: Kinsmen who are not in the direct descent line of Ego; for example, brothers, sisters, father's brother, mother's brother, father's father's brother's son.

CONSANGUINEAL RELATIVES: "Blood relatives"; relatives genetically related to Ego.

DELICT: An offense, a violation of the established law.

EDICT: A declaration of a new law or regulation by a political authority.

ENDOGAMOUS GROUP: A group whose members may marry only those individuals who belong to that group's membership; a group of people who "have to marry within" the group.

EXOGAMOUS GROUP: A group whose members may marry only those individuals who do not belong to the group's membership; a group of people who "have to marry outside" of the group.

EXTENDED FAMILY: As used in this book means any type of family extended beyond the limits of a nuclear family by the inclusion of one or several consanuineal relatives with, or without their respective nuclear families.

INTESTATE INHERITANCE: Inheritance according to established legal rules and not according to the last will (testament) of the deceased.

KAPAUKU CROSS-UNCLES AND AUNTS: Those Kapauku uncles and aunts who are of the opposite sex than that parent of Ego who forms a genealogical link between Ego and these uncles and aunts. For example, father's sister, father's father's brother's daughter, mother's brother.

KAPAUKU PARALLEL UNCLES AND AUNTS: Those Kapauku uncles and aunts who are of the same sex as that parent of Ego who forms a genealogical link between Ego and these uncles and aunts. For example, mother's sister, mother's father's brother's daughter, father's brother.

KAPAUKU PATERNAL CROSS-COUSINS: Those Kapauku paternal cousins whose first and last genealogical links with Ego (one of the cousin's parents and one of Ego's parents) are of the opposite sex. For example, father's sister's son, father's mother's sister's daughter's daughter.

KAPAUKU PATERNAL CROSS-NEPHEWS AND NIECES: Those Kapauku paternal nephews and nieces whose parent (who forms a genealogical link to Ego) is of the opposite sex than Ego. For example, brother's child (female speaking), father's brother's daughter's child (male speaking).

KAPAUKU PATERNAL-PARALLEL CONSANGUINEAL RELATIVES: Comprise Ego's siblings, father, paternal-parallel cousins (as defined below), parallel uncles (as defined above), children, paternal-parallel nephews and nieces (as defined below), as well as all paternal consanguineal relatives of the second, third, and fourth ascending and descending generations.

KAPAUKU PATERNAL-PARALLEL COUSINS: Those Kapauku paternal cousins whose first and last genealogical links with Ego (one of the cousin's parents and one of Ego's parents) are of the same sex. For example, father's brother's son, father's mother's brother's son's daughter.

KAPAUKU PATERNAL-PARALLEL NEPHEWS AND NIECES: Those Kapauku paternal nephews and nieces whose parent, that forms a genealogical link to Ego, is of the same sex as Ego. For example, brother's child (male speaking), father's brother's son's child (male speaking) father's brother's daughter's child (female speaking).

LEVIRATE: A regulation by which a widow has a right to marry a brother of her deceased husband.

LINEAGE: A unilineal consanguineal kinship group whose members can actually trace their mutual relationship from a common ancestor (the founder of the lineage).

MATRILATERAL RELATIVES: Kinsmen on the mother's side.

MOIETY: One of two subdivisions of a social group.

NUCLEAR FAMILY: A kinship group composed of father, mother, and their children.

PATRILATERAL RELATIVES: Kinsmen on the father's side.

PATRILINEAL: A type of unilineal descent by which relationship is traced through males only.

PHRATRY: A loose conglomeration of several sibs that are believed to be mutually related.

POLYGYNY: A marital union of a man with two or more women.

QUASI-GROUP: An Ego-oriented conglomerate of individuals who define their respective membership in this conglomerate in terms of their relationship to a common (central) Ego, and who intermittently form temporary unions while acting on behalf of the common Ego. Because of its Ego-orientation a quasi-group does not represent a distinct social entity (social group). Examples of quasi-groups: kindred, a Kapauku's debtors and creditors, a Kapauku's best friends.

SIB: A unilineal consanguineal kinship group whose members believe in a traditional mutual relationship but cannot actually trace it.

SOCIAL CATEGORY: An Ego-oriented conglomerate of individuals who define their respective membership in this conglomerate in terms of their relationship to a common (central) Ego, and who do not form temporary unions while acting on behalf of the common Ego. Because of its Ego-orientation it does not represent a distinct social entity (an absolutely defined social group). Examples of social categories: strangers of a Kapauku, enemies of a Kapauku, relatives and friends of a Kapauku.

SORORAL POLYGYNY: A marital union of a man with two or more women who are sisters.

SORORATE: A regulation by which a widower has a right to marry a sister of his deceased wife.

SUBLINEAGE: A subdivision of a lineage; a unilineal consanguineal kinship group whose members trace their actual descent from one of the offspring of the founder of the pertinent lineage.

TOTEM: A natural species (for example, a plant, an animal) that is believed to be mystically related to a subgroup of a society.

TOTEMIC GROUP: A subgroup of a society whose members recognize a mystical relationship to one or several natural species.

UNILINEAL: A principle of descent by which relationship is traced always through only one individual of a pair of relatives who are married to each other (for example, mother and father, father's father and father's mother), thus establishing a "single line of descent."

Metric System

Measures of Length

1 centimeter	=	0.3937 inches
10 centimeters	=	1 decimeter
10 decimeters	=	1 meter
1 meter	=	3.28 feet, or 39.37 inches
1 kilometer	=	0.62137 miles

Land Measures

1 square meter	=	1550 square inches
1 square kilometer	=	0.3861 square miles